D1561661

Alcohol, Drugs, and Arbitration

An Analysis of Fifty-Nine Arbitration Cases

BY ROBERT COULSON
WITH MITCHELL D. GOLDBERG

Published by the
AMERICAN ARBITRATION ASSOCIATION

ISBN Number: 0-943001-20-X
Library of Congress Catalog Card Number:
87-71691

Second Printing, November 1988
Third Printing, September 1991

Order from:

American Arbitration Association
140 West 51st Street
New York, New York 10020–1203
212-484-4009

Contents

Introduction

American workers consume an enormous amount
of alcohol and drugs. It has been estimated that twenty
million smoke marijuana, and millions more are heavy
drinkers. The consumption of such substances satu-
rates our society. On the job, it creates many kinds of
problems for management, including increased absenteeism and reduced productivity.

This book looks at the drug and alcohol problem
through the eyes of labor arbitrators. It is based on doz-
ens of cases decided in recent years in which unions
went to arbitration to protect the legal and contractual
rights of their members.

In the United States, members of labor unions are
protected by collective bargaining agreements that
spell out the working conditions and other aspects of
employment, establish a secure relationship between
union and employer, and provide a procedure under
which employee grievances can be resolved. Generally,
the union has the right to complain whenever it believes that one of its members has been treated unjust-
ly, in violation of the employee rights guaranteed by
the contract. If the dispute is not resolved by discussion between the union and management, it can be
submitted to an impartial arbitrator. An arbitration
hearing is somewhat akin to an informal trial, with the
employer attempting to justify its action and the union
asserting the rights of its members. The format of the

arbitration is described in the arbitration clause of the contract, which often refers to the Voluntary Labor Arbitration Rules of the American Arbitration Association (printed at the end of this book). Usually, an arbitrator is mutually selected by the parties from among the more than three thousand professional labor experts who serve in that capacity. A main source of arbitrators is the national panel of the American Arbitration Association.

In the cases in this book, arbitrators wrestle with many kinds of problems created by substance abuse. When an employee comes to work drunk, what should management do? What kind of discipline is appropriate? Is an employer obliged to rehabilitate an alcoholic or drug addict? Should an employer have the right to terminate such a worker?

What about drug testing? How accurate is it? Should such testing be required prior to employment, used on a random basis, or imposed only when some drug-related problem has arisen? Must the union consent to such testing?

The trend today is to treat drug addiction and alcoholism as illnesses. Must arbitrators follow the same line? How concerned should they be about the business needs of employers? Should an arbitrator consider the testimony of coworkers who might not want an alcoholic or drug user returned to work? What is the relationship between substance abuse and job performance?

Drugs are hardly a novelty. Their widespread use in the United States reflects in part our unique willingness to respond to the market. In answer to consumer demand for drugs, modern production techniques, combined with diabolical marketing and distribution systems, have converted drug dissemination into an extremely profitable business.

Are we doing enough to counteract the drug industry? Eighty-five percent of the $1.7 billion anti-drug budget for 1986 was spent on law enforcement. Only fifteen percent went into research, education, and treatment. Enforcement seems to have been ineffectual. Drugs of all kinds can be purchased in the street, even such obvious killers as heroin and "crack." It is no wonder that labor arbitrators are encountering drug cases with increasing frequency.

In this book, alcohol is treated as simply one more drug. True, drinking is not illegal, except for minors. Many American workers indulge in recreational drinking. Employers themselves provide alcohol to their employees at parties and other special occasions in the belief that it encourages socialization. But like other drugs, alcohol can be abused.

The cases in this book focus on the abuse. No attempt has been made to clarify the ethical distinctions between the various substances used by American workers. Crack. Grass. Booze. No matter!

Of the arbitration awards described here, forty-three were from private industry and sixteen from the public sector. They arose in various parts of the United States. Twenty-four were won by management, eighteen by unions. Twelve were something of a compromise in that while discharge was not upheld, the grievants were given a substantial penalty. Three of the cases are difficult to categorize because the grievants were put back to work, but only after successfully completing rehabilitation programs. In two cases, the arbitrators were asked to advise the parties about whether new drug policies could be instituted.

Management won most of the cases involving undercover investigators and cases where a termination was based on drug testing. Otherwise, the decisions fell almost equally on each side. Arbitrators seem to "call them as they see them." Every case is different. Neither side would be in arbitration unless it thought that it had some chance of winning.

In almost every case, the arbitrator's award is accepted by both parties as a final determination of the issues involved. In their collective bargaining contract, they have agreed to abide by that decision. The Supreme Court of the United States, in *United Steelworkers of America v. Enterprise Wheel and Car Corporation*, 363 U.S. 593 (1960), told courts to defer to the awards of labor arbitrators, provided they "draw their essence from the collective bargaining agreement." Courts have generally followed that ruling, although there is a compelling itch among some judges to second-guess arbitrators.

Such a case is *S.D. Warren Company v. United Paperworkers International Union, AFL-CIO, Local 1069*, 815 F.2d 178 (1st Cir. 1987), *vacated and remanded*, 108 S. Ct. 497 (1988). This case, referred to as *Warren I*, has been up to the Supreme Court once, and may be again. In the arbitration, Dr. Suzanne Butler Gwiazda, a Boston arbitrator, had agreed that three women working in a paper mill had violated plant rules by selling small amounts of marijuana to an undercover agent. They had been discharged. She reduced their discharges to suspensions.

The arbitrator noted that the company safety policy handbook said that violations of certain rules, including the marijuana rule, "*may* mean immediate discharge." She analyzed the company's past practice. The vast majority of such infractions had been penalized by something less than immediate discharge. Specifically, of the forty-one violations of the rules in the record, only two had resulted in immediate discharge. Both involved incarceration for serious crimes: manslaughter and incest.

After considering the facts of each case, the arbitrator reduced the employees' penalties to suspensions ranging from four to seven months. The grievants were to receive full back pay, seniority, and benefits, minus interim earnings and pay for the period of their suspensions. The arbitrator concluded that the discharges should be "overturned on the grounds that they were excessively harsh in light of past disciplinary practice for similarly serious Mill Rule 7 violations. Heavy suspensions are imposed, however, to impress upon the grievants the seriousness of their misconduct." Her award was issued on September 19, 1985.

The matter went before a magistrate in the U.S. district court in Maine, who recommended that the award be vacated on the grounds that the arbitrator had exceeded her authority. The district judge did not accept the magistrate's recommendation and confirmed the award.

This decision, in turn, was reversed by a three-judge panel of the court of appeals for the First Circuit, which concluded that the arbitrator's decision did not draw its essence from the agreement and that it violated public policy.

Judge Pieras, in the First Circuit decision, emphasized the national policy against the use of drugs in the workplace: "The nation has focused on the corrosive consequences of drug sale and use and has devoted itself to their eradication. In particular, the workshop is a place where such usage is abominable not only because of the health hazard it creates, but also because it creates an unsafe atmosphere and is deteriorative of production, the quality of the products, and competition." He pointed out that it was dangerous to use drugs in a paper mill, expressing concern about possible injuries to employees.

On the issue of contract interpretation, Judge Pieras was particularly critical of the arbitrator's opinion: "The linguistic legerdemain that this arbitrator performed was an attempt to garner more authority to herself than the parties agreed to give her. As such, she exceeded her authority."

This decision went to the Supreme Court, where it was vacated and remanded to the First Circuit for reconsideration in light of the Supreme Court's ruling in *United Paperworkers International Union, AFL-CIO v. Misco, Inc.,* 108 S. Ct. 364 (1987). The circuit court in *Warren I* assumed that *Misco* would preclude overturning the award on the basis of public policy, but held that the arbitrator, once having found a violation of Mill Rule 7, was bound by the language of the contract and the employer's decision to terminate the grievants. That decision seems questionable, since the arbitrator went to great lengths to interpret the contract language based on past practice and internal ambiguities. In a companion case, *S.D. Warren Company v. United Paperworkers International Union, AFL-CIO, Local 1069,* No. 87-1570 (1st Cir. May 19, 1988) (*Warren II*), First Circuit Judge Coffin concurred in the disposition of the particular case because of the decision in *Warren I,* but vigorously pointed out that *Misco* requires courts to give substantial deference to the interpretive findings of labor arbitrators.

Labor arbitration awards must be conclusive in order to serve the collective bargaining needs of labor and management. The parties want to resolve their grievances without being drawn into expensive litigation.

Arbitration is not inexpensive. Attorneys often are hired to represent the parties (more frequently by management than by unions). Labor arbitrators charge a daily fee for hearing a case and writing an opinion. Their fees range from $250 to $600 per day. Perhaps even more costly is the work time that the parties and their witnesses must lose. Arbitration is a contractual system, paid for by the parties.

The cases presented here were selected from the award bank of the American Arbitration Association and from other award-reporting services. In general, awards are handed down within five to six months after a grievance has been submitted to arbitration. But, as the reader will see, some of these awards were issued much later. In arbitration, delay may be caused by the parties or their attorneys, although some arbitrators do fall behind in their scheduling. The American Arbitration Association encourages arbitrators to provide early dates for hearings and to render awards promptly. Under AAA rules, arbitrators are required to issue an award within thirty days of closing the hearing.

Most of the cases in this collection relate to alcohol or marijuana, the primary substances used by working people. In evaluating the correctness of the arbitrators' decisions, the reader should bear in mind that arbitrators have broad experience in labor relations and labor law. They are not necessarily experts in drug abuse; they have been selected by the parties because of their reputation for impartiality and their understanding of the relationships between unions and employers.

Most important, the arbitrator was there when the parties presented their case, listening to the arguments of the advocates, watching the witnesses as they testified, seeing them subjected to cross-examination, deciding who was telling the truth and who was being evasive. Some of this flavor is impossible to capture in a summarized description of the case. Nevertheless, an attempt has been made to describe the relevant facts and the arguments submitted to the arbitrators in the cases in this book.

Ask yourself, as you read these cases, whether you would have come to the same conclusion. Consider, also, whether the rights and interests of the individual grievant were adequately protected.

CHAPTER 1

Employer Drug Policies and Collective Bargaining

Policies about alcohol and other drugs may be included in a collective bargaining agreement or in the employer's work rules. Such work rules often prohibit, for example, bringing certain substances into the workplace, selling or dealing in drugs, and drinking alcoholic beverages or taking drugs while on duty. Sometimes, such provisions have been negotiated into a contract because drug-related incidents have already occurred and the parties want to avoid similar problems in the future.

When a company's drug policy has been carefully formulated and clearly described, the parties may be able to apply it without any need for arbitration. Disagreements about the policy can be negotiated in collective bargaining. Carefully drafted provisions reduce the uncertainty that could otherwise create the need for filing grievances.

Questions arise when employers and unions are negotiating such provisions. Should the rules for alcohol differ from those regarding other drugs? Should penalties for violation be specified? How much discretion should an employer retain? If bringing a certain drug onto the premises is prohibited, should the rules attempt to distinguish whether it was brought there for use or for sale?

How about the employee who comes to work under the influence? How should "influence" be measured? Must the employer demonstrate that job performance was impaired or will proof of intoxication be enough to make a case? Will an arbitrator uphold an employer's unilateral right to determine what penalty is appropriate? Needless to say, there are few clear-cut cases. As the following examples illustrate, decisions about whether an employee should be disciplined are difficult to predict.

DRUNK IN A POWDER KEG

The arbitrator's decision-making authority is defined by the collective bargaining agreement. For example, most labor contracts state that an employee may be terminated only for "just cause." Specific criteria must be met before an arbitrator can sustain such a discharge.

In this case involving an employee's discharge from a munitions plant, the arbitrator, Dr. Henry L.

Sisk of Dallas, a psychologist and former professor at North Texas State University, pointed out that the company was obliged to consider "the nature of the charge, quality of the investigation, notification of the union, knowledge of the rules and the reasonableness of the rules, and the evenhandedness with which the rule in question has been administered."

The company was manufacturing live ammunition in a plant owned by the U.S. government. The grievant came to work at 7:00 a.m. on December 14, 1979, staggering and smelling of alcohol. At the request of the management, he agreed to undergo a breathalyzer test administered by the security department. Standard procedures were followed. The result of the test was a positive blood-alcohol level, .17 percent. A union official was present during the test. On the basis of the results, management decided that the employee was clearly under the influence of alcohol. He was terminated. Arrangements were made for someone to come to the plant to pick him up.

The arbitrator applied the standards previously described and upheld the discharge. The arbitrator's opinion noted that the investigation prior to discharge had been thorough. When the employee first appeared for work that morning, his superintendent saw that he was staggering and also smelled alcohol on his breath. The superintendent's observations were verified by a breathalyzer test. The results of the test were considered, as well as the observations of witnesses who had been in contact with the employee that morning. All of the evidence led to a finding that the employee was under the influence of alcohol. The union had been informed and had participated in the discussions after the superintendent made his initial observations.

The collective bargaining agreement said that "being under the influence of alcoholic beverages or drugs

while on duty . . . shall be cause for immediate dismissal." Neither the employee's awareness of the rules
nor the reasonableness of the rules was in dispute. The
rule against reporting to work under the influence of
alcohol was well known. The company was manufacturing live ammunition, so the inherently dangerous
nature of its business justified extra caution.

Finally, the company's definition of what constituted being under the influence of alcohol had been
consistently and evenhandedly applied. The company
testified that, since 1952, every employee whose blood-
alcohol level had tested .10 percent or higher had been
discharged. The arbitrator concluded that the employer
had adhered to generally accepted standards for establishing just cause for discharge. He denied the
grievance.

It might be helpful here to put this employee's
blood-alcohol reading of .17 percent into perspective.
The legal limit for driving under the influence in many
states is .10 percent. The average for those arrested for
drunk driving is close to .20 percent. According to the
National Highway Traffic Safety Administration, a 160-
pound person would have to consume eleven drinks of
eighty-proof liquor during a one-hour period on an empty stomach to register that level of blood alcohol. To
reach .10 percent, six such drinks would be required.

That is heavy drinking, which might make a person who is not an alcoholic violently ill or incoherent.
But alcoholics build up a tolerance to liquor. They
register high on the blood-alcohol scale when they turn
up for work in an intoxicated condition. This grievant
would probably have been arrested if stopped by the
police while driving. He was well over the legal limit.
The employer was wise in getting him a ride home.

Management will seldom rely on an employee's coworkers to give testimony about drug or alcohol abuse.
That kind of testimony is usually provided by supervi-

sors, security guards, undercover agents, or the police. Here, the employer had a standard provision in its collective bargaining agreement making drunkenness a cause for immediate dismissal. It was relatively easy to justify termination, based on the testimony of supervisors, supplemented by a positive breathalyzer reading.

One wonders why the union took this grievance to arbitration. What was the attitude of the union? Was a strong defense made? Or was the union only going through the motions? It is not in a union's best interests to have an alcoholic or a confirmed drug abuser working in the plant. Unions represent the interests of all of their members, not just those with behavioral problems. A union is often willing to work cooperatively with management on what it regards as a common problem. But sometimes, for political reasons, the union may decide that it has to contest a particular grievance. Then it may be convenient and useful to ask an arbitrator to decide.

Most drug-related grievances are resolved through discussions between the union and the employer, without the need for arbitration. The union can decide which grievances to contest. Perhaps that is why none of the cases in this book involves heroin or crack. The union may have no appetite for defending hard-drug cases. An individual addicted to hard drugs is often incapable of keeping a job or of sustaining the loyalty of the union.

ONE FOR THE UNION

On November 8, 1983, at about 10:00 p.m., a bus collided with a motorcycle, injuring the cyclist and his passenger. According to the bus driver, he had been forced to swerve to the left to avoid a car entering the highway from the right. At the same time, the motorcycle had moved up to pass in the outside lane.

After the accident, police officers appeared on the scene, as did supervisors from the transportation authority. The first supervisor to arrive was told by a police sergeant that the bus driver was going to be arrested on suspicion of being under the influence. The supervisor talked with the driver himself, asking him how he felt. Later, he reported that the driver spoke and moved slowly and had "glassy" eyes. The driver did not smell of alcohol.

The next supervisor to arrive, a half hour after the accident, also spoke to the bus driver. He reported that the driver's eyes were bloodshot. Again, no alcohol smell. He warned the driver that he might be arrested. Later, police officers handcuffed the driver's hands behind his back and escorted him from the bus into a police wagon. By then, the service supervisor had arrived. He too recorded that the driver's eyes were "glassy" and that he was swaying as he moved around in the bus and, later, when he was taken into the police wagon.

Based on those reports, the bus driver was discharged for being under the influence. At the hearing, he denied having consumed any alcohol or drugs. Evidence was submitted showing that his breath and urine had been tested by police from samples taken at about 3:00 a.m. on the following morning. No indication of alcohol or drugs was found. Criminal charges against the driver were dropped on January 18, 1984.

This case was heard by a tripartite panel. The neutral arbitrator, James W. McMullen, former labor negotiator for the governor of Pennsylvania, made short work of the testimony of the supervisors because it was based on fragmentary, subjective impressions. The authority objected to the laboratory evidence, but the report had impressed the arbitrator. The authority was obliged to show that the grievant's mental or physical reactions had been impaired. This it failed to do. The arbitrator pointed out that it is normal for someone involved in a serious accident to have a glazed look and to be somewhat confused. A man whose hands are handcuffed behind his back, with a police officer holding onto his belt, cannot be expected to walk in a normal manner.

The arbitrator sustained the grievance, ordering reinstatement with back pay, reduced by the driver's earnings since his discharge. The union's party-appointed arbitrator agreed. The authority's arbitrator dissented, as party-appointed arbitrators often do.

How should the supervisors have handled this case? What kind of investigation would have demonstrated that this driver was under the influence? Why did the authority disavow the urine test made by the police? Did the likelihood of the filing of a civil suit by the injured motorcyclists against the authority influence its actions? Perhaps, but this case is something of a puzzle. It is difficult to understand why the employer discharged the driver on such flimsy evidence.

Employers sometimes contest weak cases because an executive has taken a stubborn position for personal reasons, or because they think that some principle is involved, or because they have given control of the case to an outside attorney. Here, there is no clue as to why the employer persisted in what turned out to be a losing effort.

THE SAFETY FACTOR

One of the reasons that industrial employers and unions put anti-drug provisions into their collective bargaining contracts is to protect the safety of the work environment. Baker Marine Corporation was building offshore, jackup oil rigs at its facilities in Ingleside, Texas. This required the use of massive cranes and other potentially dangerous construction equipment. If equipment operators were under the influence of intoxicants, the danger would be increased.

The company has a strict drug rule: "Any employee found in possession of intoxicating beverages or drugs, or found to be drinking or under the influence of alcohol or drugs. First Violation—DISCHARGE."

The company was plagued by an increasing number of unexplained accidents. Several employees had been killed. The company's accident rate exceeded the norm in the industry. Accompanying these safety problems were concerns about extensive drug use by employees. According to the vice president for operations, employees "seemed to be using drugs prior to work, during work and during lunch breaks."

Management concluded that drug use had caused a number of the accidents. Many jobs in the yard required concentration, alertness, and an ability to react quickly. The use of drugs impairs exactly those abilities.

The presence of drugs on the premises was confirmed by an undercover drug-enforcement agent who reported "substantial drug use and possession among employees." Acting on that information, the company instituted a program to reduce drug use on the premises. During April of 1980, security police with dogs trained to sniff out marijuana were used to catch employees who brought the drug into the plant. The dogs roamed the parking lot. They would communicate the presence of marijuana by sitting on their haunches and pointing at a suspected vehicle.

The program was successful. The security police

confiscated a sizable amount of marijuana and other drugs. As the employees became aware of the possibility of detection, the amount of contraband fell off. The use of the dogs was continued on a random basis.

On May 12, 1980, the drug-sniffing dogs had been combined with security police sitting in unmarked cars. According to the company, one such guard reported that an employee was seen walking toward the plant after driving into the parking lot. After spotting the dogs, he returned to his vehicle. He next sat down in the driver's seat, made movements under the seat and the dashboard area, and threw a small plastic sandwich bag onto the ground next to the rear wheel of a pickup truck parked in the next slot. The security guard then went up to him and ordered him to pick up whatever he had thrown on the ground. Upon inspection, the contents of the bag were positively identified as marijuana. A more thorough search of the vehicle disclosed marijuana seeds. Shortly thereafter, the dogs made their characteristic positive identification of the grievant's vehicle, confirming the presence of marijuana inside the vehicle.

The grievant told a different story. He claimed that, after arriving at the parking lot, he was putting on his shirt outside of his car when the security guard rushed up to him and told him that he was "busted." The guard ordered him to pick up a package next to the truck. The grievant claimed that he had never seen the package and that it had not come from his car. He said that he never smoked marijuana. The employee was nevertheless discharged for possession of drugs. The union claimed that the grievant was being framed, either by the security guard for personal reasons or by the company because the grievant was considered a troublemaker.

The arbitrator, Ernest E. Marlatt of Houston, Texas, formerly a professor of law at the University of Houston, had to decide whether to believe the employee's testimony or a written report submitted by the security guard, who did not testify at the hearing. The arbitrator pointed out that the grievant had everything to gain from denying his guilt. His testimony was consistent with his self-interest.

The arbitrator did not accept the union's assertion that the security guard had planted the evidence to improve his reputation for getting results. "If the security guard plotted to frame the grievant, then the dog must have been his accomplice when it positively identified the recent presence of marijuana in the grievant's car. That thought boggles the mind. Was the dog also bucking for a promotion?"

The union argued that the company had discriminated against the grievant, since other employees had been treated more leniently. The union cited three cases in which employees had received no more than a suspension for marijuana possession. The company observed, however, that more than twenty employees had been terminated for drug possession. The arbitrator noted that, in one of the three cases cited by the union, no marijuana was found. In another, the marijuana had been left in the vehicle by the employee's brother. "Employers are not required to apply identical disciplinary measures for like offenses. The employer may properly consider whether more lenient discipline may serve the desired purpose of correction so that an employment relationship may be salvaged. For this reason, the company's discharge of this grievant was not discriminatory."

The arbitrator denied the grievance. But this case, unlike the previous ones, was far from open-and-shut. The result turned on credibility. Unless one attended the hearing, listened to the witnesses, and watched them as they testified, it would be difficult to decide such a case. Here, the employer was upheld, perhaps because the arbitrator felt that any company that operates dangerous machinery should be strict about drug abuse.

A NUCLEAR PLANT
IS NO PLACE FOR DRUGS

In a nuclear plant, the rules are necessarily strict. At the LaSalle Nuclear Power Station in Illinois, operated by Commonwealth Edison, the security services were provided by Burns International. A marijuana leaf was found pinned to the bulletin board in the employees' cafeteria (placed there, it later turned out, by a former guard who had been discharged). This prompted a frenzied investigation, including an unannounced search of the personal lockers of two hundred guards. The search was carried out by two of Burns' lieutenants, accompanied by union representatives. The union had agreed to the search.

Nuclear power plants are licensed and supervised by the federal Nuclear Regulatory Commission. Under Commonwealth Edison's plant rules, "contraband" was to be kept out of the protected area. This included weapons, explosives, and all nonprescription drugs. One of Burns' major responsibilities was to keep out such contraband. No wonder that the security service reacted energetically to the provocative marijuana leaf on the bulletin board.

A small bag containing fifteen to eighteen seeds was found hidden in one of the guards' lockers. When the seeds were identified as marijuana, the guard was confronted. He denied having any knowledge of the bag, claiming that at least five other guards had the combination to his locker. Any one of them could have put the bag there. One of them, he said, had been talking about growing marijuana.

The guard was asked to take a polygraph test. On the advice of his union, he refused to do so. The company suspended him and later discharged him for possession of drugs. The union filed a grievance.

The arbitrator, Duane L. Traynor, a lawyer from Springfield, Illinois, formerly a technical consultant with the Illinois State Police Merit Board and an FBI agent (1938–1946), became convinced that the grievant was responsible for the seeds in his locker. "Locker searches have never been conducted before. There is no reason to suppose that someone who had marijuana seeds would seek out the grievant's locker to hide them in. He could just as well have felt that they were safe in his own locker."

The arbitrator further stated, "By bringing marijuana into the plant and storing it in his locker, no matter what the reason, the grievant caused embarrassment to his employer, giving Commonwealth Edison an opportunity to question the ability of his employer to perform the services for which it contracted. He jeopardized the jobs of some 200 other security guards."

The union countered that the small quantity of marijuana found did not justify such a severe penalty; progressive discipline should have been employed. The arbitrator did not agree. Ever since Three Mile Island, the public has expressed deep concern regarding nuclear accidents. Operators of nuclear power stations are expected to do everything possible to assure that no failure will occur. Even a small amount of a drug, when found in a nuclear power station, justified discharge.

The arbitrator concluded that progressive discipline was not appropriate. "A nuclear power station is

not a place where such conduct can be countenanced."
He denied the grievance.

IS MARIJUANA MORE DANGEROUS
THAN ALCOHOL?

Should an employer treat the use or possession of
alcoholic beverages as seriously as it treats marijuana?
Should the severity of the penalties be the same?

On September 20, 1982, at approximately 9:00
p.m., an experienced security officer at the Mallinckrodt plant in St. Louis heard an alarm sounding in
Building 204. He was told to investigate and report
back. Upon approaching the building, he noticed an
open door. Glancing into the darkened building, he saw
three company employees, one of whom seemed to be
smoking marijuana. He asked them what they were doing in the building. Rather than respond, they walked
away, returning to their various work stations.

Later, the three men were questioned separately
by the officer in the presence of a union steward and
a company official. One of the men admitted that he
had been smoking marijuana, but afterward denied
having said it. The other two men denied having been
in the building.

Arbitrator Marshall J. Seidman, an Indianapolis attorney and former dean of the law school at Indiana
University, concluded that the security officer was telling the truth. The three employees were sharing a joint
during their break, in violation of a company rule that
subjected employees to immediate disciplinary action,
including discharge, for possession of drugs while on
company premises. The arbitrator took the word of the
officer over that of the three grievants.

Seidman then considered whether discharge was

the appropriate penalty. This award has often been cited by other arbitrators on the issue of whether the penalty for smoking marijuana in the workplace should be substantially the same as for drinking on the job.

Inconsistent application of a drug policy might persuade an arbitrator to overturn disciplinary action. The employer's obligation to treat employees with fairness and consistency is frequently mentioned by arbitrators discussing drug and alcohol abuse in the workplace. A union may attempt to show such inconsistency where a work rule does not discriminate between drugs and alcohol.

In this arbitration, the union showed that in several recent cases involving possession or use of liquor on company property, the penalties imposed were one-day, three-day, and two-week suspensions. After several such suspensions, one employee was discharged because his alcoholism was causing excessive absenteeism. Even that employee was later rehired, contingent upon completion of a rehabilitation program.

This evidence convinced the arbitrator that the company customarily used progressive discipline when enforcing alcohol abuse. In no case had an employee been discharged for a first offense of alcohol abuse. The union contended that discipline for marijuana should be the same as for alcohol. Progressive discipline should be applied.

The company attempted to justify its more severe approach toward marijuana. Marijuana is illegal. The use of marijuana is more difficult to control. Marijuana users may become psychologically dependent on a "euphoric state approaching sensory derangement."

Seidman wrote an opinion reviewing the attitudes of other arbitrators on this issue, referring to many awards between 1973 and 1982. In more than two-thirds of the cases in which an employee was terminated for marijuana use, the discharge was set aside for being excessive and the grievant was reinstated without back pay. Of those cases, four dealt with the issue of whether the punishment for marijuana abuse should be consistent with the punishment for alcohol abuse. In all four, the arbitrators agreed that this should be so.

Seidman noted that marijuana and alcohol share some similar properties: each can lead to psychological dependency, mind alteration, and the risk of degenerating to more severe dependence. Employee job performance can be impaired by either alcohol or marijuana. He added that alcoholism in industry is a far more debilitating, costly, and destructive social problem than marijuana. There is no reason to treat them differently. It was therefore improper to treat alcohol abuse with progressive discipline while responding to marijuana abuse with immediate discharge. Seidman said that the company had failed to show why legality was a relevant factor. There was no proof that the illegality of marijuana affected plant safety or efficiency.

The arbitrator concluded that discharge was excessive. He ordered that the three workers be reinstated but refused to award them back pay. They were guilty of using marijuana during their break. They lied and continued to lie throughout the investigation and the arbitration. They should not be allowed to profit from their abuse of the system. "To obtain justice one must act justly."

Which is more debilitating, alcohol or marijuana? The answer depends on many factors—the job, the degree of substance abuse, the individual's ability to control the habit, and the setting in which the use occurs. In the cases that follow, some employees are devastated by substance abuse, while others continue to operate on its recreational fringes. Alcohol or marijuana? There is no easy answer as to which is more debilitating, but it is clear that both create problems in the labor–management setting.

DRIVE A TRUCK ON FIVE BEERS A DAY?

Don Lee Distributors is a beer wholesaler. It acquired another company, with the understanding that the employees would be hired if they passed a physical examination given by the purchaser's physician. The issue in this case was whether an acquiring company had to offer employment to a driver–seller suffering from an alcohol-induced liver disease.

The purchaser's physician recommended that the driver be denied employment. His examination had revealed an enlarged liver associated with drinking problems. The employee had a record of alcoholism. He afterward had a physical examination administered by his own doctor, however, which found no evidence of liver disease and offered no reason why the employee could not drive a truck. The company nevertheless refused to hire him. His union filed a grievance.

The company claimed that it was not obliged to continue the driver's employment. "An employer who knows that an employee is an alcoholic need not wait until disaster strikes before acting."

The grievant testified that he drank five or six beers a day. He said that he never drank on the job or reported to work under the influence. At no time during his fifteen years with his previous employer had he ever been disciplined. The union also argued that, under the acquisition agreement, employees had to be offered a job unless the examination showed a "severe health problem," a "life-threatening situation." Neither was present in this case. The union argued that prior alcoholism should not be grounds for termination. The company had to show that the grievant's drinking affected his job performance, which it had failed to do.

The arbitrator, Dr. Jack Stieber, a law professor at Michigan State University, agreed with the union. When a discharge is reviewed by an arbitrator, it must be justified by the fact that the grievant's drinking affects his performance in the workplace. An addiction to alcohol often manifests itself in diminished job performance—either excessive absenteeism or reduced productivity. The company had not produced evidence that the grievant's drinking had ever affected his work performance.

The issue here was whether the company had just cause to refuse the grievant his contractual right to continued employment. This was not a case of a new hire applying for a job. In most situations, job applicants can be rejected even if the employer only suspects that they drink or use drugs. So, although the company would "not be faulted for refusing to hire a new employee who had a drinking habit similar to that admitted by the grievant," there was no just cause for terminating this employee, absent evidence that the drinking affected his job performance. The company was directed to reinstate the grievant.

SOBERING UP
IN THE OHIO RIVER

This employee was a deckhand for the Ohio River Company, which runs barges on that river. Barge crews are on board for twenty-five days, with twenty-five days off. When on board, they work six hours on and six hours off.

The deckhand joined a pusher vessel in the afternoon of December 13, 1983. Instead of signing the boarding report at once, as is customary, he worked loading stores. He then went to bed, asking the captain if he could switch with another hand as the swing man. This was agreed. During the night, he went up to the bridge to tell the pilot that he had failed to complete the boarding report because he forgot his glasses. They had a friendly conversation. He completed the report on the following day.

At about 6:00 p.m., while the vessel was going through a lock, the deckhand was called out to help with the barges. Somehow, he fell overboard, sustaining serious injuries. The hospital to which he was taken reported that he had been heavily intoxicated. His blood-alcohol level was found to have been .3034 percent, which, according to the doctor, was high enough to render a normal man unconscious.

The following day, the deckhand admitted that he had been drinking. He was discharged pursuant to a posted company rule prohibiting the consumption of alcohol on company vessels. "Any violation of this rule will result in immediate suspension, possibly resulting in discharge."

The arbitrator, Thomas L. Hewitt, a lawyer from Latrobe, Pennsylvania, said that the case turned on the word "possibly," which indicated that the company intended management officials to consider various factors in determining whether termination was appropriate. In reducing the discharge to a 60-day suspension, the arbitrator took into consideration the grievant's participation in Alcoholics Anonymous. He also looked at the grievant's work record, which contained no history of disciplinary action for at least eight years.

Hewitt pointed out that other members of the crew knew that the grievant had been drinking. They covered for him when they should have notified their supervisors. "Alcoholism is a disease, and can be corrected. Practically the only accepted method in industry is through alcoholic rehabilitation involving Alcoholics Anonymous and usually a stay in a rehabilitation center or hospital." He emphasized that management had a duty to enforce its rules against drinking and to follow up when employees were discovered drinking. Management had failed to "consistently apply the no alcohol rule in all situations on all vessels." If rules are not applied, employees do not expect strict enforcement.

Hewitt said that he did not mean to suggest that other employees could drink with impunity until they are caught and then join Alcoholics Anonymous. Each case must stand on its own. Discharge might be appropriate in other cases; in this case he gave the grievant another chance.

Under cross-examination, this employee was asked whether he regarded himself as an alcoholic. "Well, I would say I was. But I ain't now." Perhaps he was not. His good work record would indicate that he might be a good candidate for rehabilitation.

AN EMPTY BOTTLE OF BEER

On May 5, 1983, an employee was seen by three supervisors placing a brown paper bag on the ground in the company's parking lot. They walked over and collected the bag, which contained a quart bottle, still cold, with an inch of beer remaining at the bottom. The supervisors reported the incident to the general foreman, who immediately called in the employee to discuss the situation. The employee said that he drank the beer during his thirty-minute trip to work. Thinking that the bottle was empty, he then tossed it under the truck of a coworker.

The employee was suspended, pending discharge, for violating the company rule against "reporting for work in unfit condition such as under the influence of alcohol, or possession of an alcoholic beverage on company property." A subsequent letter stated that he had been seen "with an open quart bottle of beer in your hand from which you were observed drinking."

The employee had eight years' seniority, but a poor record, including two warnings for sleeping and a thirty-day suspension. There had been no previous problems with alcohol.

The testimony of the three supervisors at the hearing indicated that none actually saw the grievant drinking beer. The arbitrator, Marvin J. Feldman, an attorney from Cleveland, Ohio, ruled that the employer had failed to prove its case. There was no evidence of drinking or being unfit for work. The arbitrator found that just cause was not demonstrated by the evidence. The employee was reinstated with full back pay.

SUMMARY

Many collective bargaining agreements and work rules prohibit drug or alcohol possession or use and strictly define the applicable procedures for discipline or for rehabilitation. Arbitrators are governed by such language. Federal or state laws might also be applicable.

Drug and alcohol abuse cases raise a common question: did "just cause" exist for the action taken by the employer? As with other discipline cases, an arbitrator must consider whether the grievant had notice of the rules, whether the rules were fairly applied, whether the charges against the grievant were adequately investigated, whether the grievant had a reasonable opportunity to answer the charges, and whether the discipline fit the offense. The employer has the burden of proof and must come forward with the evidence. The definition and application of the term "intoxication" or "under the influence" may have to be determined.

In cases involving alcohol, the standards for determining whether these terms apply are reasonably well established. The presence of alcohol can be measured by breathalyzers or by urine or blood tests. For certain jobs, employers may forbid the consumption of any alcohol within a prescribed period of time, under penalty of discharge and regardless of any question of impairment. This is true, for example, in airlines, ground transportation, and other activities where everyone, including the public, is committed to safe operation. There, the employer's standards may be particularly rigorous.

In addition to chemical tests, workers can be considered intoxicated because of their appearance, slurred speech, bloodshot eyes, or unsteady gait. These criteria are often part of the proof presented by an employer, particularly when the bargaining unit is relatively small and testing facilities are not readily available. For example, a school teacher who comes to work smelling of alcohol might be disciplined after the school nurse smells it on his or her breath, while a technician in a large industrial corporation might be taken off to a hospital in the company ambulance for a full-blown workup by a test laboratory.

The use of marijuana and other drugs may be more

difficult to demonstrate through subjective observations by members of supervision. There, drug testing may be necessary. What test to use? How to administer such a test? These have become important questions for corporate management.

An arbitrator will listen to the evidence on such issues in whatever form presented by the employer. The union must try to demonstrate that the evidence is inadequate, contradicted by other testimony, or misleading. The next chapter discusses exactly that question—the question of proof.

CITATIONS

Drunk in a Powder Keg: Day & Zimmermann, Inc. *and* International Chemical Workers Union, Local 526, 75 *Labor Arbitration Reports* (LA) 699 (1981).

One for the Union: Southeastern Pennsylvania Transportation Authority *and* Transport Workers Union, Local 234, AAA Case No. 1439-0173-84 (unpublished).

The Safety Factor: Baker Marine Corporation *and* United Steelworkers of America, Local 8237, 77 LA 721 (1982).

A Nuclear Plant Is No Place for Drugs: Burns International Security Service, Inc., LaSalle Nuclear Power Station *and* International Union, United Plant Guard Workers of America, Local 235, 78 LA 1104 (1982).

Is Marijuana More Dangerous than Alcohol?: Mallinckrodt, Inc., St. Louis Plant *and* United Automobile, Aerospace and Agricultural Implement Workers of America, Local 1887, 80 LA 1261 (1984).

Drive a Truck on Five Beers a Day?: Don Lee Distributor, Inc. *and* International Brotherhood of Teamsters, Local 1038, 312 *Summary of Labor Arbitration Awards* (AAA) 6 (1985).

Sobering Up in the Ohio River: Ohio River Company *and* United Steelworkers of America, Local 14262, 83 LA 211 (1985).

An Empty Bottle of Beer: Consolidation Coal Company Burning Star No. 4 *and* United Mine Workers of America, Local 1825, 295 AAA 9 (1983).

CHAPTER 2

Problems of Proof

In alcohol and drug cases, an employer must be able to convince the arbitrator that the alleged violation took place. What standard of proof do arbitrators require? Will they be satisfied with the kinds of proof generally accepted in civil litigation or in other labor arbitration cases, or will they demand a more rigorous standard, more akin to that of a criminal proceeding?

Arbitrators' rulings on these questions may vary on a case-by-case basis. In some situations, the arbitrator must determine which party has the burden of proof. Take, for example, the issue of impairment, the inability to do one's job.

While bizarre behavior, bloodshot eyes, and other signs of abnormality might indicate that a person is under the influence of drugs, actual impairment is difficult to prove. The technologies of urinalysis and blood testing are still in their infancy. Impairment is difficult to establish by objective standards. Some collective bargaining agreements specify that a reading of 100 or more for metabolites of THC is proof of impairment from marijuana use. But drug tests only record usage. They do not establish the degree of impairment. Moreover, marijuana stays in the body tissue and can still be revealed by urinalysis several weeks after use.

In most arbitrations, the initial burden to demonstrate a violation of the established work rules falls on the employer. Arbitrators might accept credible testimony by a plant manager or supervisor as being sufficient to shift the burden of proof to the union. The grievant must then do more than simply deny the accusations in order to shift the burden back to the employer.

An arbitrator might require a higher standard of proof to sustain a discharge than for a lesser punishment. Testimony from a company official without corroboration from some third party could be insufficient. It is difficult to forecast exactly how much proof an arbitrator will require in a given case. Termination—full loss of employment—is the most serious industrial penalty. An arbitrator will usually want to be certain that the alleged conduct occurred and that termination was warranted.

Alcohol and drug cases raise common questions, although the evidence introduced may vary in emphasis. Detailed and corroborative testimony about physical behavior, job performance records, medical and drug identification reports, and impairment tests may be required. Symptoms of intoxication are frequently introduced in alcohol cases—for example, bloodshot or glassy eyes, slurred speech, incoherence, excessive perspiration, belligerence, and insubordination. In contrast, where the charge involves the use of drugs, physical symptoms and disruptive behavior are less frequently introduced into evidence. The primary proof is likely to be the sworn testimony of supervisors or security personnel. In alcohol cases, the symptoms of intoxication can establish use. In drug cases, a company representative may have had to observe the grievant using the drug.

Sometimes, an arbitrator will sustain a grievance where the employee can demonstrate that the symptoms were caused by medication. In other cases, the behavior of the grievant, combined with a refusal to take a drug test, will persuade the arbitrator to deny a grievance. Sobriety tests can play a prominent role in the outcome of alcohol cases. Arbitrators have to decide how much weight to give to such tests. The technology is fairly well established. Drug tests, on the other hand, have been given less credence. Cases dealing with such tests are discussed in Chapter 3. Here, it is enough to say that where there is some reasonable belief that an employee was using drugs or alcohol, refusal to submit to a test could be considered evidence of such use.

The degree of proof required in arbitration is frequently a factor, particularly in testing cases that involve the use of illegal drugs. Some arbitrators require "clear and convincing" proof rather than a "preponderance of the evidence." A higher standard might be appropriate where there is uncertainty about the scientific accuracy of the test as proof of impairment and about the difficulty of quantifying such a test. The cases in this chapter involve questions of proof. How can one convince an arbitrator that an employee violated the work rules and should be punished? How much proof is required? What evidence will an arbitrator accept?

CAUGHT IN THE ACT

A typical drug possession case involved an employee of Shenango China. The company had a rule against possession of narcotics or illegal drugs on company property. The general foreman saw an employee sitting at a table rolling what appeared to be a cigarette. He approached the employee, who dropped what was in his hand onto a plate and covered it with a newspaper. The foreman then reached under the newspaper and pulled out the plate. On it was a package of rolling papers and a small amount of a substance that looked like marijuana. He took the plate back to his office and put its contents into a plastic bag, which he taped shut. He then called the manager of industrial relations.

After his supervisor was consulted, the employee was given a five-day suspension, pending discharge. The penalty was read to him with his shop steward present. The employee was then escorted from the plant. He was later discharged.

At the subsequent arbitration, both the foreman and the manager of industrial relations testified that they were familiar with marijuana as a result of attending training programs given by the state police. The confiscated substance had been tested by a laboratory and photographed. Sure enough, it was marijuana. All of this testimony and evidence was submitted to the arbitrator.

Although the grievant denied that he had been rolling marijuana, the arbitrator, Robert A. Creo, of Pittsburgh, a graduate of Washington University School of Law, was convinced that an infraction had taken place. He noted that several prior warnings and suspensions appeared on the grievant's record. The grievance was denied.

The proof here was well presented. The supervisor immediately took control of the material and maintained the integrity of the chain of custody. In other cases in this chapter, problems of proof become more complicated.

ONE HIT AND ONE MISS

Arbitrators expect evidence to be clear and convincing before they will sustain a discharge. This case involved two workers who were caught smoking marijuana in a secluded passageway at a sugar factory. The plant engineer discovered the two electricians smoking a "hand-rolled and somewhat crumpled cigarette with the end twisted." He recognized the aroma of marijuana and noticed that the cigarette was held by one of the workers in a "roach clip."

After warning the men that he would have to report the incident and being asked not to do so, the plant engineer reported to the foreman. Both of them hurried back to the alcove. The odor of marijuana there was pronounced. They immediately informed the shop steward of the incident. Since only one replacement electrician was available, they sent the man who had been holding the cigarette home but allowed the other to finish his shift.

On the following morning, both employees were discharged for violating a plant rule prohibiting "drinking or having in one's possession intoxicants or narcotics on plant property." The union argued that the evidence did not support the company's claim that marijuana was what the employees were smoking. Both men denied that the substance was marijuana. The one who had held the cigarette claimed that it contained tobacco and that he had held it with needle-nosed pliers because the filter was damaged.

Circumstantial evidence convinced the arbitrator that the grievants were not telling the truth. They had been in a secluded passageway, some distance from their workplace. This was not where workers would go to smoke an ordinary cigarette. The man holding the cigarette was holding it in "the fashion common to marijuana smokers rather than to smokers of ordinary tobacco cigarettes." Moreover, the grievant had testified that he smoked marijuana two or three times a week, although never in the plant. Both the plant engineer and his shift foreman had identified the smell. No reason was given why they would not be telling the truth.

The arbitrator, Professor Emeritus Leonard Oppenheim of Tulane University, explained that all of the circumstances considered together presented a convincing case that the grievant possessed and had used marijuana. The discharge of the employee holding the cigarette was sustained.

Because the other grievant had not been observed smoking, his case was different. Although he had been with a man who was smoking marijuana, the company failed to provide clear and convincing evidence of his guilt. Management had allowed him to finish his shift, indicating that the company had considered him "physically and mentally capable of working the rest of his shift, that is to say he did not appear drugged. Otherwise he would have been sent home too."

The arbitrator concluded that only the employee actually caught with the marijuana should be terminated for just cause. The other was reinstated. One hit and one miss.

A HOT LUNCH BOX

Another marijuana case involved a plant rule at the Amoco Oil Company that any employee who brought intoxicants into the refinery or reported for duty under the influence would be suspended or discharged without prior notice.

An employee was terminated after marijuana was found in his lunch box. Many of the facts were undisputed. On November 26, 1981, the employee clocked out of the refinery and went to the parking lot. Realizing that he had forgotten his keys, he set his lunch box down beside his car and went back to the plant. When he returned, the lunch box was gone.

The box was later turned in at the guardhouse. For over fifteen hours, it remained in the window of the guardhouse to be claimed by its owner. Finally, one of the guards opened the box to search for identification. Inside, she found a book and fourteen grams of marijuana in a brown paper bag. The marijuana was positively identified by an expert witness. The guard was told by her supervisor to report the name of anyone who asked for the box.

On the following day, the owner came to claim his lunch box. He was asked to open the box and examine its contents. When questioned about the paper bag, he denied any knowledge of its contents. The guard told the employee to write down his name and number but he refused, leaving without his lunch box.

Later, at a meeting with the operations superintendent, the employee was questioned about the marijuana. He denied ownership of either the book or the bag, explaining that he had refused to give his name to the guard because he was scared. He denied being a marijuana user, noting that he was a "health freak" and ran long distances. At the conclusion of the meeting, he was given an indefinite suspension. Later, he was notified of his termination. The letter explaining the employer's position stated that "the company believes that you knew the marijuana was in your lunch box and you knowingly had possession of marijuana on company premises. This was an extremely serious incident."

The arbitrator, Dr. F. Jay Taylor, president of Loui-

siana Tech University, decided that the weight of the
evidence, while sufficient to justify a lengthy suspension, was not enough to sustain discharge. The evidence was largely circumstantial, admissible but insufficient to justify the harsh penalty given. He pointed
out that arbitrators require a strict standard of proof
in drug cases. "I must have before me substantial and
irrefutable proof that he was indeed guilty of the culpable act."

The arbitrator admitted that the grievant was probably guilty. "It well may be that he is receiving a lesser
penalty than he deserves. But this happens many times
in the American system of justice when a guilty party
goes unpunished. The standard of proof necessary to
sustain conviction is simply lacking."

The arbitrator pointed out that the company had
not been damaged in any way. There was no evidence
that the grievant used marijuana. He was described as
a good or average employee with no prior record. On
the basis of all of the facts, Dr. Taylor reduced the termination to a suspension. The grievant was to be re-
stored to his job within ten days of the receipt of the
award, but without back pay. This added up to a suspension of seven months.

NOW YOU SEE IT,
NOW YOU DON'T!

In this case, a garage employee was terminated for
drinking alcohol during working hours, in violation of
company rules and policies. On October 17, 1983, three
supervisors caught four employees sitting around a
table in a room at the rear of the garage. While looking
through a peephole, one of them had seen the grievant
put a styrofoam cup to his mouth. The grievant then

dropped the cup below table level, as if to hide it. On the table at the time was an open bottle of whiskey, a bottle of soda water, and two or three cups. Only the grievant was seen drinking.

All of the employees were told to punch out for the day. The supervisors testified that the room smelled of alcohol, but none of them had smelled the cups.

The grievant denied drinking any alcohol. He maintained that he had been in the room because he was looking for his crew chief to receive a new assignment. Three other employees also were in the room at the time. One admitted to drinking. The second denied it. The third took the Fifth Amendment.

The grievant, who had a poor employment record, was discharged. The other three employees received thirty days' probation, with two weeks off without pay. Their prior records, a factor in their milder penalty, had been better than that of the grievant, who had recently received ninety days' probation for a "serious infraction of the rules and policies" of his employer.

A grievance relating to that discipline was still pending, so the parties agreed to submit it to the same arbitrator, George T. Roumell, Jr., a partner in the law firm of Riley and Roumell in Detroit. The earlier infraction involved the grievant's alleged failure to report a traffic accident involving a company van, in which the grievant was a passenger, and his presence in an unauthorized area. Roumell decided that the grievant was culpable in this earlier incident.

Circumstantial evidence of the kind presented here is scrutinized carefully. The evidence in this case did not prove that the grievant actually was drinking liquor. He might have been drinking soda water. The supervisors had assumed that liquor was in the cup. No evidence that the grievant was under the influence of alcohol was submitted. No analysis was made of the contents of the cups. In cases involving termination, an employer is expected to carry out an investigation to show that the violation has occurred. None had been conducted.

The arbitrator ruled that the employer had failed to produce sufficient evidence to warrant discharge. If one of the supervisors had smelled liquor in the grievant's cup, the circumstances would have shown that he was drinking. If they had actually seen him drinking liquor, the result would have been different. Arbitrators will uphold discharges based on drinking on company premises, but proof of the drinking must be presented. Roumell was not satisfied with the proof in this case but felt that for being in a room where alcohol was being consumed, the employee should receive some punishment. He should not have stayed in the room. He knew that he was in the wrong place at the wrong time. The arbitrator reduced the termination to a sixty-day suspension without pay, still a stiffer penalty than the other three employees received. This was reasonable, based on the grievant's poor work record.

Since the award was issued more than a year after the incident, the employer had to reimburse the grievant for six months of back pay. "Candidly," Roumell concluded, "this arbitrator is not overjoyed in awarding any back pay on the unusual circumstances of this grievance. Because of his past work record, the grievant has an obligation to stay away from anything even suggesting liquor while on agency time and on agency premises."

UNDER THE INFLUENCE?

A difficult task in alcohol cases is to determine at what point the individual came "under the influence" and was therefore subject to disciplinary action. How does the employer show that an employee is under the influence? Arbitrators sometimes look to state law for the definition of what constitutes "under the influence." But since those guidelines are established to define criminal offenses, an arbitrator is not required to defer to them. An arbitrator may decide to apply a different standard, perhaps one that is more rigorous. In this case, however, the Georgia motor-vehicle law was relied upon to resolve the grievance.

A bus driver with the Metropolitan Atlanta Rapid Transit Authority (MARTA) reported to work on December 5, 1984. Her superior smelled alcohol on her breath. The grievant admitted to drinking two "California Coolers" two hours and fifteen minutes prior to reporting for work. An alcohol test administered by an industrial clinic indicated a positive blood-alcohol level of .04 percent. The driver was terminated for violation of a company rule:

Rule 11—Intoxicants or Drugs
Section A—The drinking of intoxicants or the use of drugs that intoxicate are prohibited when used less than twelve hours before reporting for duty, while on MARTA premises or while in uniform at any time. . . .
Section C—An employee found to be in possession of or under the influence of intoxicants or illegal and dangerous drugs, including marijuana, while reporting for duty, while on duty or on MARTA premises will be discharged.

The grievant had admitted to a violation of Section A, drinking less than twelve hours prior to reporting to work. It was not clear whether she had also violated Section C by being under the influence of intoxicants when reporting for duty.

To arbitrator C. Gordon Statham of Decatur, Georgia, a former FBI agent, this distinction was important. Violations of Section A were merely "prohibited," while Section C required that violators "be discharged." Statham pointed out that MARTA had a legal and moral obligation to protect the safety of its passengers. It had consistently discharged employees who failed blood-alcohol tests.

It was necessary to determine whether the grievant had been under the influence of intoxicants and, therefore, subject to immediate termination. Statham relied on a Georgia motor-vehicle statute that read, "If there is at any time .05 percent or less by weight of alcohol in the person's blood, it shall be presumed that the person was not under the influence of alcohol as prohibited by sections 1, 2, and 3 of code Section 46.39." The grievant's blood-alcohol level of .04 percent was below the level of the Georgia statute.

There being no other evidence to indicate that the driver was under the influence of alcohol, the arbitrator decided that discharge was too severe. The grievant did, however, violate Section A. Since the incident had occurred some ten months before the date of the award and the grievant had been suspended without pay, the arbitrator ordered the company to reinstate her with her prior seniority but without back pay, with a one-year probationary period.

DRUNK OR UNDER MEDICATION?

Some companies have no procedure for testing alcohol or drug consumption. In such situations, the determination of whether or not an employee is under the influence may be based on the observations of supervision. The following case is typical, except that the employee claimed that his strange behavior was caused by a prescribed medication.

The grievant had been working for over sixteen years at various custodial positions within the District of Columbia's school system. Recently, he had been promoted to assistant engineer custodian of Parkview Elementary School. His responsibilities included cleaning the school building and maintaining the heating system.

On January 26, 1979, the school's principal noticed that the grievant seemed to be agitated and disoriented. She testified that he took short steps, walked hesitantly, and was wearing dark glasses inside the building. The principal was concerned enough to contact the area manager, telling him that the grievant seemed "spaced out."

The area manager went to the cafeteria, where the grievant was mopping the floor. According to his later testimony, the custodian was working in a sluggish fashion. His speech was slurred. When he removed his glasses at the request of the manager, his eyes seemed bloodshot.

The grievant said that all of these effects were due to medication. The manager concluded that the grievant was unfit for duty and should be sent home. The conversation between the two men became heated, with the manager threatening to call the police if the grievant did not leave the school grounds.

On February 1, the grievant was discharged for having reported to work under the influence of alcohol or drugs, being unable to perform his duties, insubordination, and disregard for standards of conduct. He denied that he had been under the influence of alcohol. He claimed that he had a painful ear infection and was using Darvon, a prescribed painkiller, to relieve his discomfort. In the past, Darvon had made him drowsy but did not disable him if he stayed active, as his job required.

Was the evidence sufficient to support management's conclusion that the grievant was under the influence of alcohol or drugs? Neither the principal nor the area manager had smelled alcohol on the grievant's breath. The manager testified that, since the grievant was responsible for boilers, it seemed safer to send him home. There was no indication that the grievant had ever been under the influence of alcohol during his lengthy term of employment. Two other employees testified that on the day of the incident he had seemed normal.

The arbitrator, Louis Aronin, a former deputy director of the Office of Labor Management Relations of the U.S. Civil Service Commission and an adjunct professor at Georgetown Law Center, noted that the grievant had not shown any of the customary symptoms of chronic alcohol or drug abuse. On three earlier occasions, he had been disciplined for absences without leave. On four others, he was disciplined for insubordination or failure to carry out a work assignment, but never for chronic absenteeism or incapacity.

Aronin felt that the grievant's testimony about the side effects of Darvon was consistent with the *Physician's Desk Reference*: "When Darvon is taken as directed, side effects are frequent. Among those reported are drowsiness, dizziness, nausea, and vomiting. If these effects occur, some of them may go away if you lie down."

Based on that evidence, Aronin concluded that the grievant's symptoms might have been caused by Darvon rather than alcohol or drugs. The employer would not have terminated the grievant for drowsiness associated with Darvon, a prescribed medicine. Not having been provided with any contrary medical testimony, the arbitrator had to accept the grievant's explanation that Darvon had caused his problems. He found no basis to conclude that the grievant's use of medication constituted a purposeful commission of any improper act. He reinstated the grievant with full back pay.

The board of education presented a remarkably thin case. None of the witnesses testified that they smelled alcohol. No physical examination was carried out. No prior evidence of drug or alcohol use was demonstrated. Perhaps management felt that the grievant's poor work record would carry the day. If so, they guessed wrong. In order to win such a case, solid evidence will be required.

It took seventeen months in this case to obtain the arbitrator's award. Large metropolitan school systems and their unions sometimes accept lengthy delays in their grievance and arbitration procedures. When such delay becomes chronic, the parties should evaluate their grievance procedure and identify the cause.

SUMMARY

The cases in this chapter indicate what is required to prove drug or alcohol use. Some of the grievances were upheld, others denied. What made the difference? What standard of proof did the arbitrators demand? Which party has the burden to provide evidence? Will testimony about erratic behavior be enough, or will some form of testing be necessary? What are the differences between proving cases involving "under the influence," as compared to "possession" or "use"?

When discipline is called for, it is important that supervision be prepared to take decisive and effective action. But the union should also be involved. Drugs and alcohol are a concern for both union and management. Unions are eager to resolve such situations, particularly where plant safety or the company's reputation is involved. Union members do not want their jobs threatened because a few employees indulge in drugs or alcohol. Sometimes, management has the mistaken idea that the union is not concerned about drug use. That is seldom the case. Often, the union is just as worried about such situations as the employer. This point often emerges when the employer wants to institute a drug-testing program. The next chapter contains some interesting cases on exactly that subject.

CITATIONS

Caught in the Act: Shenango China, Division of Anchor Hocking Corporation *and* United Steelworkers of America, Local 3125, AAA Case No. 5530-0178-83 (unpublished).

One Hit and One Miss: Godchaux–Henderson Sugar Company, Inc. *and* Amalgamated Meat Cutters and Butcher Workmen of North America, Local P–1124, 81-1 *Labor Arbitration Awards* (ARB) ¶ 8090 (1981).

A Hot Lunch Box: Amoco Oil Company, Texas Refining Company *and* Oil, Chemical and Atomic Workers International Union, Local 4–449, 9 *Labor Arbitration Information System* (LAIS) 1207 (1982).

Now You See It, Now You Don't!: Maintenance Central for Seniors *and* American Federation of State, County and Municipal Employees, Michigan Council 25, AAA Case No. 5439-0457-84 (unpublished).

Under the Influence?: Metropolitan Atlanta Rapid Transit Authority *and* Amalgamated Transit Union, Local 732, 86 *Labor Arbitration Reports* (LA) 334 (1986).

Drunk or under Medication?: Board of Education of the District of Columbia *and* American Federation of State, County and Municipal Employees, District Council 20, *Arbitration in the Schools* (AIS) 128-15 (1980).

CHAPTER 3

Testing for Drugs or Alcohol

Drug testing is a relatively recent phenomenon, but one of growing interest. Labor arbitrators are hearing more and more drug abuse cases. When an employer must prove that an employee was under the influence of drugs or has been using drugs, testing can provide the major part of an employer's case.

Legal precedents about drugs and alcohol in the workplace are still evolving. Some of the cases in this book involve situations where the grievant may be a defendant in a criminal court at the same time that an arbitration is taking place between the union and the company. This can cause conflicts. Arbitration decisions are not binding upon the courts but may have an impact. On the other hand, the union and the employer may decide to suspend the arbitration until the criminal case is resolved.

How will arbitrators react when drug-testing programs are created by employers? Will mandatory drug testing be regarded as an invasion of personal freedom?

Where employees are represented by a union, drug and alcohol testing is usually considered to be a mandatory subject of bargaining. An employer may not install such a program without giving the union an opportunity to bargain over its effects. Both sides are likely to be concerned about the reaction of the workers. However, they might be surprised at how many employees would welcome drug testing. Arbitrators might be surprised as well.

Drug testing is becoming a common issue in arbitration. Two recent awards in sports make the point. Arbitrator Tom Roberts, of Rolling Hills, California, was asked whether professional baseball teams could institute drug testing without bargaining with the players' association. The collective bargaining agreement contained a "zipper" clause providing that no amendments could be made without further negotiations. Roberts ruled that the unilateral introduction of drug testing was prohibited during the term of the contract.

In the National Football League, arbitrator Richard Kasher, who has served on five presidential advisory boards, decided that commissioner Pete Rozelle exceeded his authority when he ordered random drug testing for all league players. When the contract had been renegotiated in 1982, the parties had bargained over drug testing. They agreed to allow testing during the preseason physical examination, with additional testing only for "reasonable cause." "Spot checking" for chemical abuse or dependency was prohibited. The arbitrator, therefore, did not allow the NFL to add two unscheduled tests during the regular season. That would have violated the agreement.

Both arbitrators decided against drug testing. No one should have been surprised. With the current concern about drug abuse, collective bargaining agreements and work rules will increasingly contain provisions about drug testing, describing how testing will be carried out after a drug-related incident (an accident, for example) or providing for drug testing at various stages in the employment relationship. Several of the cases in this chapter deal with that subject.

Recently, the American Medical Association House of Delegates approved a report by its Council on Scientific Affairs that on-the-job drug testing should be limited to situations where there is reason to believe that job performance is impaired and to pre-employment examinations for jobs affecting the safety and health of others. Employers were encouraged to initiate such testing and to use positive test results to motivate employees to seek help for drug or alcohol problems through employee-assistance programs.

Drug testing poses difficult questions about the integrity of tests and the reliability of the techniques used by testing laboratories. For example, the popular urinalysis screen for marijuana is relatively inexpensive, but it is unreliable under even the best of circumstances. If the results are positive, they must be confirmed by a more sophisticated and expensive test— gas chromatography/mass spectrometry, which is considered reliable if done by a reputable laboratory.

Problems also arise concerning the circumstances under which a sample was obtained and its chain of custody. These concerns are particularly difficult in the case of urine testing. Must samples be collected under supervision's watchful eyes? That could be embarrassing! The idea of supervisors watching workers fill specimen jars has an air of unreality. Or will selected members of the corporate staff come to specialize in that unappealing task? If a test has to be validated, witnesses must verify every step in the process.

As drug testing becomes common, a brisk business in "clean" urine specimens will develop. One arbitrator has already had to decide whether a hospital laundry worker who substituted another person's urine for her own could be terminated for her deceit. The woman was an admitted cocaine addict and had used drugs on the job. An earlier grievance had been resolved on the condition that she enroll in a rehabilitation program and submit to random urine testing to confirm that she was drug free.

During a routine visit to her drug counselor, she was asked to leave a urine specimen. When she spilled some of her sample, she asked another woman who claimed to be drug free to add some urine to the specimen. The combined specimen showed traces of methadone. When the grievant admitted what she had done, she was fired for falsifying a record. The union did not condone her action but claimed that termination was too harsh a penalty.

The arbitrator, Alan R. Rothstein, pointed out that the grievant took a calculated risk: "She cut the final thread that bound her to her job and gave the employer adequate justification to sever the relationship" (*Hospital and Institutional Workers Union, Local 250, and Service Employees International Union* and *Ata Bates Hospital*, July 9, 1986).

Drug testing is being used increasingly by employers. Is that because laboratories and computers have improved testing technology? Is it because of the Reagan administration's stern admonitions about drugs? Or is there a growing concern about the extensive use of drugs and alcohol in the American workplace?

The drug-testing industry has prospered as business managers have come to believe that testing is an appropriate response to their drug problems. Consultants have become available, encouraging testing programs and advising on how tests can best be instituted. Medical centers offer testing facilities and laboratories have become available for the analysis of blood or urine specimens.

Drug testing now involves a highly competitive marketplace, a growing industry. The marketing efforts of potential vendors seek to persuade private organizations and public institutions to install testing programs or to use testing to confirm drug use. As in any such endeavor, there is a need for quality control. Where to turn for a reputable consultant, for medical service, for reliable testing and analysis? Where to find accurate information about the technology?

Even though many employees support the idea of drug testing, they expect management to provide accurate, reliable results. At an arbitration hearing, the union representatives may critique the testing procedures used by the employer. The arbitrator must determine through credible evidence whether the specimen was obtained, delivered to the laboratory, and tested in accordance with appropriate procedures. The results must be justified by the employer. As drug-testing cases become increasingly common, arbitrators are acquiring experience in handling those issues.

Corporations are screening job applicants and testing employees for drugs more frequently than ever before. Urinalysis can identify drug users. It can also be expensive, intrusive, and, sometimes, mistaken. It raises difficult legal issues about individual privacy. What is fair? What is legal?

Testing job applicants causes the fewest problems, since the person being tested is voluntarily seeking employment with that firm. When employees already on the payroll are asked to submit urine or blood specimens, more difficult questions arise. How can testing be justified? What is the impact on employee morale? Sensitive judgments must be made about which employees to test and how tests should be administered.

Highly technical questions arise about the accuracy of the tests. If an employee tests positive, should a second sample be subjected to a more reliable and expensive procedure? What degree of proof will an arbitrator accept? Is the risk of drug abuse worth the expense and aggravation of a testing program?

There is no doubt that random drug testing is an invasion of privacy, involving a risk that erroneous judgment calls will be made. If a company's personnel policies are intended to build trust between the workers and the employer, the installation of random drug testing could well have a jarring effect.

Indiscriminate employee drug testing is being reviewed by the courts. The federal testing program has already been stalled by recent cases. It would not be surprising to see severe limitations placed on such testing in the future. The process of requiring urine samples entails a direct assault on personal modesty.

When shown by a proper test, the presence of drugs can establish a basis for discipline. Some arbitrators believe that the presence of illegal drugs demonstrates a propensity for the use of drugs. In some employment settings, that alone could justify termination. When the grievant is an airline pilot, bus driver, police officer, or firefighter, an arbitrator may give the benefit of the doubt to the employer on grounds of public safety. If the person tested is in a less dangerous occupation, for example a clerical or food-service employee, proof of actual impairment might be required. Drug users may be offered an opportunity to participate in a rehabilitation program or be given another test a few weeks later.

Many workers use drugs on a "recreational" basis. That complicates the problem. Does an employer have the right to discipline employees for off-duty conduct? That question will be considered in Chapter 4. The nature of the employment is relevant. Employers involved in public safety or national security may have the right to test employees for drug use whenever they can show a connection between the effects of drug use and the requirements of the job. Other employers might not have such wide latitude.

Since private companies are using drug testing more frequently, it is not surprising that public agencies are doing the same. Such public employees as police officers, firefighters, and security personnel are held to a high standard. Most people would agree that they should be drug free. Many drug-testing programs have been installed by local governments. Are they legal? The courts will have to decide that question.

Government employees have special protections. The Fourth Amendment prohibits unreasonable searches and seizures by government officials. This could be interpreted to include the testing of body fluids. The leading court case is *Schmerber v. California*, 384 U.S. 757 (1976) (blood test as a violation of the Fourth Amendment). In determining whether a search is reasonable, courts apply a balancing test. The government's reason for conducting the search is weighed against the constitutional rights of the individual. Testing public employees for drugs and alcohol has been upheld where there has been a reasonable suspicion of wrongdoing or where a high-risk job is involved and public safety is at issue. For example, the courts have upheld the testing of bus drivers after accidents where the driver was suspected of being under the influence, based on the need to protect the public.

Indiscriminate drug testing raises other issues. A federal district court in New Jersey ruled, in *Capua v. City of Plainfield*, 643 F. Supp. 1507 (D.N.J. 1986), that the city violated the rights of firefighters and police officers by compelling them to submit to urine tests, absent any suspicion that particular employees were using illegal drugs.

In *Capua*, the city had ordered a surprise urinalysis. The procedure was repeated three times, until all 103 employees of the fire department had been tested. Police officers were tested at the same time.

Sixteen firefighters tested positive and were suspended without pay. They were neither given a copy of the lab report nor told what the test results showed. The city had no prior proof that any of them was using drugs. The firefighters had no advance notice that such tests would be required.

After the employees sued the city under the Civil Rights Act of 1871, the court put the suspended workers back on the job and prohibited further urine testing. Judge H. Lee Sarokin held that indiscriminate drug testing unlawfully intrudes on employees' right to privacy in violation of the Fourth Amendment and infringes on their right to due process under the Fourteenth Amendment. Later, the court enjoined the city from testing without some reasonable suspicion that a particular employee had used illegal drugs. "A urine test done under close surveillance of a government representative, regardless of how professionally or courteously conducted, is likely to be a very embarrassing and humiliating experience," said the judge. "Furthermore, compulsory urinalysis forces [employees] to divulge private, personal medical information while the government has no countervailing legitimate need for access to this personal medical data." The city, admittedly, had a legitimate interest in preventing drug consumption by employees involved in vital public-safety functions, but the court held that mass drug testing is an inappropriate way to achieve that goal.

Another federal district court, in *Allen v. City of Marietta*, 601 F. Supp. 482 (N.D. Ga. 1985), upheld the testing of six electrical workers by the city, because they were doing hazardous work on high-voltage wires. All six tested positive for the presence of marijuana after being "fingered" by an informer planted among them by the city. The informer had seen them smoking marijuana and had actually smoked with them on occasion. The court held that, as long as the testing is work related, a public employer has the same right to provide a safe, productive, and drug-free working environment as has a private employer.

Private employers are not subject to the Fourth Amendment. Other avenues of redress are, however, available. Collective bargaining agreements, private employment contracts, and various theories of tort law could provide causes of action. Defamation of character and infliction of emotional harm can justify lawsuits even in the absence of a protective statute. Because this branch of the law is still developing, these avenues may well expand in coming years.

The cases that follow show how labor arbitrators have responded to drug-testing programs. They also suggest how drug testing might affect our lives in future years.

A BLOOD TEST
TO CONFIRM INTOXICATION

Large corporations are usually methodical about obtaining evidence in cases involving "under the influence." The following is typical. Georgia–Pacific is a major paper producer. On March 13, 1984, a technician came to work at 7:00 a.m. and went about her task of performing tests and collecting samples in various parts of the mill. At 8:30, while walking through the bleach plant, she skidded on some ice and hit her head against the wall. While she was receiving first aid, the nurses smelled alcohol on her breath and reported her to management. The company had a rule against reporting for duty under the influence of liquor. Violating it could justify immediate discharge.

The technician was taken by ambulance to a hospital for a blood-alcohol test. The analysis was conducted by an independent laboratory and showed a blood-alcohol level of .189 percent. She was given a thirty-day suspension. A grievance was filed.

The union maintained that the grievant was not intoxicated. None of the management personnel who saw her that morning had said that she seemed under the influence. The union suggested that perhaps the alcohol in her blood was from a medicine she was taking, a 42-percent-alcohol elixir for bronchitis.

The issue was whether the grievant had reported for work under the influence. David R. Bloodsworth, the arbitrator, who is assistant director of the Labor Relations Research Center at the University of Massachusetts in Amherst, concluded that she had. Except for the blood test, this employer might not have been able to persuade an arbitrator that this employee was under the influence. Not only did the grievant have alcohol on her breath, but the test results established substantial intoxication. The grievant admitted that she had consumed four or five alcoholic drinks the night before but said that she had been taking an ounce of terpin hydrate and codeine per hour around the clock. Bloodsworth denied the grievance.

TESTING THE CHRISTMAS SPIRITS

Sometimes, even the most elaborate testing fails to convince an arbitrator that employees were under the influence. In this case, three employees on the night shift were suspected of drinking alcohol and using marijuana. Shortly after 9:00 p.m. on the day after Christmas, employees on that shift were all given urine tests. The three employees showed high blood-alcohol levels, ranging from .11 percent to .16 percent. Under the Ohio Motor Vehicle Law, .10 is the level that creates a presumption of being under the influence. The employer discharged all three for reporting to work under the influence of intoxicants. Their union filed a grievance.

The grievants admitted that they had been drinking during the Christmas holiday. One said that he had had six drinks, but stopped drinking at 5:30 a.m., ten hours before he went to work. Another had been drinking beer up to two hours before reporting to work. The company denied that it had tried to trap the employees by scheduling the tests on the day after Christmas.

The union claimed that the tests were unreliable. And the company had offered no evidence of intoxication other than the tests. The employees came to work in the afternoon. The company had waited until 9:00 p.m. to collect specimens. Because of the delay, the company's medical witness had to use a technique called "retrograde extrapolation" to calculate what their blood-alcohol levels were at 3:00 p.m., applying an average rate of reduction of .015 percent. By this computation, the expert decided that they were intoxicated. The union emphasized that there was no evidence that the grievants' performances were impaired.

Arbitrator Roland Strasshofer, Jr., a practicing attorney in Chagrin Falls, Ohio, wrote a comprehensive opinion. The issue was whether these grievants reported for work under the influence of intoxicants. He agreed with the union that there should have been independent corroboration of intoxication. The case turned entirely on the test results.

After analyzing several earlier arbitral awards on

the subject as well as law review articles, Strasshofer concluded that the company had not met its burden of proof. Urinalysis tests are known to be unreliable. The rate of absorption varies among individuals depending upon size, weight, stomach contents, and whether the body has become accustomed to alcohol. The effects of alcohol also vary. After alcohol is absorbed into the bloodstream, it is processed in the kidneys and excreted gradually into the bladder. The rate at which alcohol is eliminated from the blood varies from about .01 to .02 percent per hour, averaging .015.

Many medical experts recommend that a first specimen of urine should be taken and discarded to clear the bladder and a second obtained about a half hour later. Otherwise, the test is unreliable. Urine allowed to collect in the bladder over a period of several hours is history. Only fresh urine accumulating during the most recent thirty minutes will reflect the current level of blood alcohol.

Here, the grievants had consumed substantial amounts of alcohol during the holidays. That mixture which had accumulated in their bladders was what was tested. The test results did not necessarily reflect their blood alcohol at the time they reported to work. The arbitrator therefore upheld the grievances, ordering that the employees be returned to work with full back pay. The lesson for employers is to provide independent evidence of impairment and to be certain that urinalysis tests are taken from relatively fresh samples.

A FALLEN WORKER—A FAULTY TEST

Arbitrators must determine whether the particular test relied on by the employer to justify disciplinary action was accurate. Which test was given? How was it administered? How were the results presented?

This grievant was a maintenance helper with Ohio Ferro-Alloys, which produces silicon metals through an intense heating process. In March of 1982, he was working on an overhead beam, sixteen feet above the plant floor, when he suddenly fell. After first-aid treatment, he was taken to a nearby hospital.

A preliminary examination showed that he had suffered a concussion. He remained at the clinic overnight. A blood sample was taken and sent to an independent laboratory for analysis, to determine whether the employee had been drinking prior to the accident. The test showed a blood-alcohol level of .44 percent— a level that is uniformly classified as being thoroughly under the influence. A volume of .30 percent renders an individual "stuporous," and .40 percent makes one "anesthetized." Medical experts consider any blood-alcohol content above .40 percent to be "life threatening." Someone of the employee's body type would have had to drink a fifth of whiskey to reach that blood-alcohol level. The employer's case was based entirely on the result of the test.

The problem facing the arbitrator, James J. Odom, Jr., an attorney from Birmingham and former professor of economics at the University of Alabama, was that the grievant had not shown any symptoms of such an extraordinary level of alcohol. Nothing in his behavior that morning had warned anyone of his condition. Nor did the employer attempt to justify the testing process. Neither the nurse who drew the blood nor the technician who carried out the test was present at the hearing. Nor had the grievant been given an opportunity to take another test.

Undisputed testimony showed that the grievant had driven his motorbike over thirty miles to work that morning. His coworkers had seen nothing unusual in his behavior. He had climbed up to the "I" beam, high above the ground, and had been working there for some time prior to the accident. Neither two coworkers who were on the scene after the accident, nor the personnel manager, nor the attending physician at the hospital smelled alcohol on the employee's breath or noticed any unusual behavior. On the contrary, the doctor at the hospital reported that he was "alert, well oriented, and quite cooperative."

The union simply contended that the grievant had not been drinking. The issue was purely factual. The inconsistencies between the test results and the uncontested description of the grievant's behavior were too obvious for the test to be given credence. The employer had offered no testimony or witnesses as to how the test was conducted. The arbitrator, therefore, rejected the test results, and the grievant was reinstated with full back pay.

A CHANCE FOR A
SECOND TEST?

A bus driver for the Washington Metro Area Transit Authority had an accident on January 24, 1983. Afterward, she was subjected to blood and urine tests. Evidence that the test was positive was made through the testimony of the toxicology supervisor of the Washington Hospital Center and another expert witness. They described the tests and showed an unbroken chain of custody. They did not explain why the laboratory had delayed five days in reporting the results.

Eight days after the tests were administered, the driver was advised that drugs had been found in her system at the time of the accident. She then went to her personal physician to be retested, and those tests were negative.

The union contended that the results of the first test might have been incorrect. The grievant denied having taken any drugs. The accident, she claimed, was not her fault but was caused by a defect in the bus.

The arbitrator, Herbert N. Bernhardt, a professor at the University of Baltimore School of Law, pointed out that the second test taken by the grievant was irrelevant because it was conducted several days after the accident. The results did not reflect her condition at the time of the accident. The delay in taking the second test, however, was due in part to the fact that she was not advised of the initial test results for eight days.

There was a possibility that the first test was faulty, but Bernhardt thought that this had to be weighed against the harm that could result from allowing an employee who takes drugs to continue to operate a bus. The grievance was denied, but the arbitrator directed the employer to offer the grievant an opportunity to enter the authority's drug-rehabilitation program while continuing employment in a nondriving position. She was given thirty days to accept that offer.

An employee should be given the results of a positive drug test in time to obtain a second test to confirm or rebut the evidence. If not, an arbitrator would have to rely entirely on the employer's evidence. As we have seen, neither blood nor urine tests is infallible.

THIS DRUG TEST FLUNKED THE TEST

During 1984, the transportation officer of the District of Columbia school system estimated that more than sixty percent of the workers were using drugs and that this use was growing. In order to curb this trend, the board decided to require a urinalysis screen during the annual physical that was mandatory for each worker.

The grievant in this case was a school bus attendant working with handicapped children, a job he had held since 1970. On July 17, 1985, he took his physical, including the drug screen. He tested positive for marijuana. Although he denied having used this drug, he was suspended for thirty days without pay. A second test on November 2 was negative.

The union's primary argument was that the testing procedures in the clinic were defective. No follow-up test had been given to ensure the reliability of the urinalysis, even though this was specifically required by a directive issued by the school superintendent.

There are many reasons why a urinary drug screen might be wrong, including human error such as equipment contamination or sample mislabeling. Therefore, it is customary for tests to be confirmed by alternative methods that rely on a different property of the substance in question. This is done to increase confidence in the results. Even with a second test, the error rate may be as high as two to three percent, depending on the test and the laboratory.

In this case, arbitrator Jerome H. Ross, formerly assistant director of mediation of the Federal Mediation and Conciliation Service, ruled in favor of the union: "Persuasive bases exist for disregarding the results of the grievant's urine test. This record of proceedings contains no evidence regarding the testing procedures used in obtaining the grievant's urine sample and little evidence as to collection, storage and chain of custody of the sample. Most troublesome is the lack of evidence of a confirmatory test having been run on the grievant's sample in accordance with Directive 205.1.

. . . All we have in the record is a piece of paper, generated by a computer not linked to a testing instrument, with the entry 'POS/50' which has no significance."

Ross analyzed the board's regulations, pointing out that they were aimed at on-duty impairment. The board was attempting to show that a positive urinalysis meant that an employee was under the influence on school premises. In this case, the arbitrator did not accept that statement. There was no evidence of abnormal behavior. The union's expert, Dr. Arthur J. McBay, had testified that the active constituents in marijuana impair functions for only two to four hours. The inactive constituents remain in the body for a longer period of time. Ross cited technical publications confirming that opinion. He concluded that the lack of evidence about the testing procedures and about the employee's behavior required that the grievance be sustained, returning the grievant to his position with full back pay.

An employer who intends to rely on an outside laboratory to demonstrate drug use or being under the influence had better be certain that the lab follows proper procedures, that it provides confirmation tests, and that it is prepared to testify or provide credible written reports for submission to an arbitrator. There is enough difficulty in proving the reliability of urinalysis without compounding the problem by using an unqualified testing laboratory.

IS REFUSAL TO TAKE A DRUG TEST GROUNDS FOR DISCHARGE?

The grievant in this case worked in a plant that manufactured power-control devices. Her work entailed the use of hazardous machinery and materials.

She had a record of extended absences related to her use of barbiturates. On the morning of March 24, 1981, after reporting to work, she was seen "wobbling, unsteady, and staggering down the aisle." Earlier that morning, she had asked the union steward to park her car in the company lot. He was concerned enough about her condition to report it to a supervisor.

Based upon the observations of company officials and the union steward, the employee was taken from her station because she was suspected of being under the influence of drugs. She was escorted to the nurse's station, where she waited for almost an hour before the manager of industrial relations arrived. Her speech was slow and slurred. The manager asked her to take a drug-screen test. He told her that her refusal might result in disciplinary action, possibly in termination. Despite his warning, she refused to take the test.

On the following day, the employee was discharged. The company's stated reasons were her past drug problems, her condition on March 24, and her refusal to take the drug test. Later, an arbitrator was appointed to decide whether it was reasonable for the employer to conclude that she had been under the influence of drugs. Did the company have the right to order her to take a drug test to determine whether she was fit to work?

Among her extensive absences caused by barbiturate use was a medical leave lasting from June 17, 1980, through March 23, 1981. She had returned to work just one day before the incident that led to this grievance. The union argued that there was insufficient evidence that the grievant was under the influence of drugs. She did not drink and only used prescription medicine.

The arbitrator, Jonas B. Katz, an attorney from Cincinnati, Ohio, rejected the union's arguments. The employee had acted like someone who was under the influence. In light of her recent problems with barbiturates, it was reasonable for the company to suspect that she was under the influence of drugs. She was staggering and disoriented. Her eyes were glassy and her speech slurred. The fact that the grievant's problems involved the use of prescription medicine was immaterial.

Katz cited the decision in *Porcelain Metals Corporation*, 73 LA 1133 (1980), where arbitrator Raymond Roberts said, "The prohibition is clearly designed with a twofold purpose. First and foremost, it is a safety rule to protect both the employee who might be under the influence of drugs and his fellow employees from harm and injury. Secondly, it is designed to protect the company against paying wages to an employee who is incapable of performing productively with reasonable efficiency. Given these two clear purposes of the rule, it is immaterial whether the drug is prescriptive and its possession is legal or illegal."

Based upon the grievant's poor employment record, her behavior on March 24, and her refusal to submit to the test, the arbitrator found that the company was justified in terminating her employment. He denied the grievance.

DOES MOUTHWASH SMELL LIKE ALCOHOL?

When the grievant, a porter for Trailways Bus Company, returned from lunch on November 22, 1983, he was called over by his supervisor to receive a work assignment. The supervisor smelled alcohol on the porter's breath. The employee explained that he had eaten a hamburger while walking back to work. He said that he always removed his dental bridge before eating. Afterward, he had used mouthwash to avoid trapping food particles under his bridge.

The company's manager suggested that the porter accompany him to a nearby hospital to take a blood-alcohol test. At first, the employee agreed. On the way to the car, however, he changed his mind, saying that he was dirty and wanted to go home and take a bath. The supervisor and the manager tried to persuade him, but he continued to refuse. When they all returned to the manager's office, the employee asked that his shop steward be present. He continued to refuse to go to the hospital, explaining that he had a lawyer's appointment that afternoon at 2:00 p.m. The lawyer, whose name the porter would not divulge, was to defend his nine-year-old son in criminal court on the following day.

The manager ordered the employee to go to the hospital for a test. Finally, the man agreed to go in his own car. The two company officials also drove to the hospital. Once there, the porter asked an attendant how long he would have to wait before a technician would be available to administer the blood test. When the attendant answered that he did not know, the porter walked out, saying that he could not wait any longer. He proceeded to his appointment with the lawyer. When he returned to work on the following afternoon, he was suspended for drinking during work hours and for insubordination. He was later discharged. A grievance was filed that went to arbitration.

This case again raises the question of whether an employer can presume that an employee was under the influence of alcohol because of a refusal to be tested. The union argued that such a presumption was improper here: the employee had a legitimate concern for his child. The fact that the porter had an afternoon appointment with his attorney was not in dispute; his son had been charged with larceny. The hearing had been scheduled for the following day.

The arbitrator, Robert G. Williams, an attorney from Charlotte, North Carolina, who formerly taught law at the University of North Carolina, pointed out that the blood-alcohol test would not have interfered with the grievant's ability to attend his son's trial. He concluded that the grievant had tried to hide behind the appointment with the lawyer to avoid taking the test.

The company rule in this case provided that no employee shall "report for duty, go on duty or remain on duty when under the influence of any alcoholic beverage or liquor, regardless of its alcoholic content, or with the odor of same on their breath; nor shall any employee drink any such beverage while on duty, on lunch break periods or within six hours of reporting for work." As Williams put it, proving a violation of such a rule can be "an uncertain experience." The company had a right to ask for a blood-alcohol test to prove its case. By refusing to take such a test, the employee established a reasonable presumption of guilt. The arbitrator denied the grievance.

HOW TO INSTALL DRUG TESTING IN A UNION PLANT

On February 18, 1982, the Griffin Pipe Products plant in Lynchburg, Virginia, posted a notice informing all employees that a drug test requiring urine specimens would be administered to employees who reported for medical treatment. There was also a reminder about the established rule against "drinking, possession or use of any alcoholic beverages or drugs on company property or being under the influence of drugs on company property." At the same time, the company made a drug-screen test part of its pre-employment physical examination. The tests were administered by the company doctor and paid for by the company. The specimens were shipped to Biomedical Laboratories in North Carolina. Results were usually obtained in two to three days.

The union grieved the new procedure on behalf of the members of the bargaining unit, claiming that it was overly broad and unclear as to its objectives. The union said that such a test was disciplinary.

In applying the new procedure, employees who tested positive would be suspended—not as a disciplinary measure, according to the company, but nevertheless without pay. The employee could not return to work until testing negative. The company noted that the results of the test would not go into the employee's file. It attempted to justify the procedure on the ground that there had been rumors of drug use on one of the foundry's shifts. The company's primary motivation, however, seemed to be that similar tests were being used successfully in other facilities.

The arbitrator, J. Harvey Daly, explained why the case was unusual. There were no individual grievants. He was being asked to evaluate a procedure, not necessarily to enforce a contractual right. The issue was whether the new drug-testing procedure was reasonable. He found that it was.

IS TESTING A BARGAINING ISSUE?

This case involves a challenge by the union to a drug and alcohol procedure that the Bay Area Rapid

Transit District (BART) intended to adopt for train operators, station agents, and certain other employees in San Francisco's rapid transit system. The union filed a grievance before the procedure went into effect. Arbitrator David A. Concepcion, former associate dean of Hastings Law School, had to decide whether BART needed the union's approval and whether the procedure was consistent with the contract.

Whether bargaining was required hinged on a provision in the contract stating that BART would not unilaterally change any rules, regulations, or practices affecting the "beneficial" rights of the employees. The union said that the right of the employees not to be subjected to drug testing was a beneficial right.

Concepcion brushed aside that argument. Previously, there had been no procedure for drug testing. He felt that BART had the right to implement a new procedure as part of its management rights, particularly in view of the long-standing rule against alcohol or narcotic abuse (Rule 107). He pointed out that any new drug procedure had to be reasonable. Concepcion then carefully analyzed the new procedure, which provided for testing whenever supervision felt that an employee might be under the influence of alcohol or drugs.

Rather elaborate provisions were included as to how to implement testing. Concepcion found several flaws in the procedure. Its purpose was to control employees who were under the influence of drugs or alcohol while on duty, based on the need for safety and efficiency. Ninety-five percent of the employees in the unit dealt with the public or performed work in which safety could be a factor. But Concepcion pointed out that the drug-testing requirement also included the five percent who did not. In addition, other aspects of the procedure were unreasonable. For example, BART should not be allowed to charge an employee with insubordination for refusing to consent to the test. Nor should a refusal to take the test stand alone as proof of being under the influence.

He discussed the kinds of tests that might be offered. An employee should have the right to select the best available test and to subject a portion of any sample to independent testing. The procedure should also include verification testing. The union had claimed that it was unreasonable for BART to call in the police when an employee refused to be tested. Concepcion agreed, although the use of police might be appropriate in some cases if the situation got out of hand.

Since several parts of the new procedure seemed unreasonable, Concepcion sustained the grievance, rescinding the procedure but allowing BART to issue a proper procedure in the future. In the alternative, the parties could negotiate the terms of a testing procedure.

SUMMARY

Drug testing of job applicants is being used by both private and public employers. A recent survey of major police departments by the National Institute of Justice (NIJ), *Employee Drug Testing Policies in Police Departments*, reported that twenty-four out of thirty-three had such programs. Sixty-three percent of the departments screened officer applicants for drug use, rejecting candidates who tested positive. In some cities, more than one-quarter of the candidates tested positive.

Twenty-one percent of the departments test probationary officers. Thirteen percent test officers being transferred into vice, narcotics, or other sensitive bureaus. Seventy-five percent test those suspected of drug abuse. There was no reported policy of random testing of all officers, although one department combines drug screening with the annual physical.

Most public agencies with drug-testing programs use a two-part process. The Enzyme-Multiplied Immunoassay Technique (EMIT), which is inexpensive but less accurate, is confirmed by the more accurate gas chromatography/mass spectrometry test. "Even when both tests are used, a possibility remains that 'false positives' will occur," the NIJ report cautions, so most departments investigate further.

Drug testing has become a common feature in the American workplace. Some employers do not require screening for new hires. Others make it part of accident investigations. Still others require testing when employees are suspected of coming to work under the influence or are discovered using specific drugs.

How are such tests best administered? How should the results be used? How should testimony about testing be presented to an arbitrator? How accurate are such tests? Where can one find a reliable laboratory for testing samples? Where does one get information on the technology?

The cases in this chapter have illustrated some of the common problems facing arbitrators who must decide cases that turn on testimony about the various drug tests. It is also important to remember that none of these tests tells where the abuse took place. Nor are they very exact about the time at which the drug was taken. Drug use usually occurs during off-duty hours. That is the subject of the next chapter.

CITATIONS

A Blood Test to Confirm Intoxication: Georgia–Pacific Corporation, Woodland Division *and* United Paperworkers International Union, Local 27, AAA Case No. 1130-1273-84 (unpublished).

Testing the Christmas Spirits: Chase Bag Company *and* Amalgamated Clothing & Textile Workers Union, AFL-CIO and Bag Workers Union, Local 377T, 331 *Summary of Labor Arbitration Awards* (AAA) 11 (1986).

A Fallen Worker—A Faulty Test: Ohio Ferro-Alloys Corporation *and* United Steelworkers of America, 285 AAA 9 (1982).

A Chance for a Second Test?: Washington Metropolitan Area Transit Authority *and* International Brotherhood of Teamsters, Local 922, 11 *Labor Arbitration Information System* (LAIS) 2017 (1984).

This Drug Test Flunked the Test: Board of Education of the District of Columbia *and* American Federation of State, County and Municipal Employees, Council 20, Local 2093, *Arbitration in the Schools* (AIS) 202-14 (1986).

Is Refusal to Take a Drug Test Grounds for Discharge?: American Standard, Wabco Division *and* International Brotherhood of Teamsters, Chauffeurs, Warehousemen and Helpers of America, Local 651, 77 *Labor Arbitration Reports* (LA) 1085 (1982).

Does Mouthwash Smell Like Alcohol?: Trailways, Inc. *and* Amalgamated Transit Union, AFL-CIO, Local 1531, 312 AAA 5 (1985).

How to Install Drug Testing in a Union Plant: Griffin Pipe Products Company *and* United Steelworkers of America, Local 2864, 288 AAA 9 (1983).

Is Testing a Bargaining Issue?: Bay Area Rapid Transit District *and* Amalgamated Transit Union, Division 1555, *Labor Arbitration in Government* (LAIG) 3819 (1986).

CHAPTER 4

Off-Duty Abuse

Many arbitrators think that an employee's private life should be of no concern to the employer. Therefore, an arrest for drug or alcohol use or possession away from the employer's premises should not justify disciplinary measures unless the arrest prejudices the employer's public image or the employee's work performance.

Professor Harry Shulman, the late dean of Yale Law School, put it this way:

> We can start with the basic premise that the company is not entitled to use its disciplinary power for the purpose of regulating the lives and conduct of its employees outside of their employment relationship . . . . What the employee does outside the plant is normally no concern of the employer. If the employee commits no misconduct in the plant during working hours, he is not subject to disciplinary penalty, though he may beat his wife, spend his money foolishly, or otherwise behave like an undesirable citizen.

When a worker abuses alcohol or drugs during nonworking hours, at home or anywhere else away from company premises, an employer, in order to take disciplinary action, is obliged to connect the drug use to the employee's job responsibilities. Sometimes, however, drug abuse leads to criminal sanctions or other complications that disqualify the employee from further employment. The chaotic shadow world of the drug user or confirmed alcoholic may become incompatible with steady employment. Those situations illustrate the emotional torment endemic in this kind of lifestyle.

Some employees work in such sensitive environments that they must be totally above suspicion, both on and off company premises—for example, correctional workers who counsel former drug abusers, security guards in nuclear power plants, and members of police narcotic squads. It is important for the protection of society that these workers be drug and alcohol free.

ONE LAST CHANCE

An all-too-common situation involving alcohol abuse is the employee who goes to prison for drunk driving. If unable to work for an extended period of time, can such an employee be terminated by the company?

That situation occurred in the U.S. Envelope Division of Westvaco. The grievant was a working foreman on the swing shift. He had fourteen years' seniority, with no record of absenteeism or other discipline. He did have a drinking problem.

In 1983, he was arrested for driving under the influence. He asked the court to enroll him in an atabuse program to control his alcoholism (atabuse is a substance that causes illness when combined with alcohol). He was refused, however, because his work brought him into contact with substances containing alcohol that would have made him sick. He was given an eighty-day jail sentence. The employee requested a leave of absence from work to serve his sentence. The company refused, terminating him on the basis that he would be unable to perform his job.

The arbitrator was Adolph M. Koven, a well-known mediator and educator from San Francisco. Koven pointed out that some arbitrators have upheld discharges for absence caused by incarceration, on the theory that an employee is obliged to be available for work. But he felt that where the absence is involuntary, as it was here, it should be excused. Most arbitrators reject that argument when the employee is incarcerated for a willfully committed crime. "No employee goes to jail voluntarily . . . but people are responsible for their actions, or should be." In general, incarceration has not been accepted as an excuse for missing work.

Arbitrators usually consider the reason for incarceration, the length of the sentence, the impact on the employer's operations, the employee's work record, past practice, and any special circumstances. Koven compared the facts in this case with other arbitration awards. He pointed out some relevant factors. Here, there was long service and no evidence that the employer would suffer. In addition, the conviction was in no way related to the business.

Chronic alcoholism is a disease. Arbitrators have generally held that the alcoholic is entitled to a chance for rehabilitation, particularly a long-service employee. Koven decided that discharge was too severe. He ordered the grievant reinstated without back pay.

WHAT URINE TESTS
DON'T PROVE

Three employees of the board of education of the District of Columbia were suspended after they tested positive for marijuana pursuant to a National Health Laboratories EMIT screen test of their urine. The grievants all testified that they did not use marijuana themselves, but had been socializing with people who did. All three of the employees were disciplined for violating Superintendent's Directive 662.13, which prohibited the possession, use, or being under the influence of narcotics or other drugs, such as LSD, marijuana, and the like, on school premises.

Arbitrator Roger P. Kaplan of Washington, D.C., pointed out that the grievants had not been charged with using drugs on school premises. He went on to discuss the validity of the urinalysis test. The manufacturer of the EMIT test, Syva Corporation, advises customers to confirm initial findings with alternative procedures. The EMIT test was developed to be used as a presumptive screen, not to independently support disciplinary action. Testimony introduced at the hearing indicated that substances other than marijuana might affect the results of the test. In this case, all three grievants tested negative in their second urinalysis, lending credence to the unreliability of the EMIT test. In any case, that test does not determine how much marijuana is in the urine, when it was consumed, or how it was consumed. Any discipline based solely on an EMIT test would be questionable; in any case, however, off-duty use of marijuana, even if proven, would not establish a violation of the regulation. The grievances were sustained, with the employees receiving full back pay.

This case involved alleged off-duty use of drugs. Therefore, even if the use had been demonstrated, it is unlikely that an arbitrator would uphold the discipline. An employee's behavior away from the job is generally considered that person's own business. The employer has no right to intrude.

But what is off duty? Is an employee off duty while in a car parked in the company lot? How about during a lunch break? What about off-duty behavior that affects job performance? There is no easy answer to these questions.

A DRUG TEST FOR THE NIGHT SHIFT

The employer here was a food-product distributor. In August of 1984, management became aware that alcohol, marijuana, amphetamines, and cocaine were being used on company premises during working hours. Acting on professional advice in an effort to eliminate drug abuse, the company told certain employees on the night warehouse shift to submit to a urine test designed to detect the presence of alcohol and drugs. Chosen for testing were employees who had been named in an informant's reports, who operated heavy equipment, or who worked closely with either of those groups.

A one-day notice of the company's intention was given to the union. Urine samples were collected the next day. Two employees refused and were suspended, one of whom was ultimately discharged. The other later gave a urine sample, which tested negative, and he was reinstated. Of the eighty-nine samples collected, ten tested positive for marijuana. The affected employees received a notification that read as follows:

Please be advised that your urinalysis tested positive for an illegal or controlled substance. We want to insure your continued employment with CFS Continental, Seattle, and, in lieu of discharge, we want to give you every opportunity to cease the use of any and all illegal drugs. Therefore, as a condition of continued employment, you must elect one of the two following options:

(1) Consult a recognized drug rehabilitation counselor for evaluation. You must authorize release of the counseling report to the company. Following the counseling and evaluation, you will undergo another urinalysis in sixty days; however, if the test is positive, you will be discharged.

(2) You may elect to have another urinalysis test immediately and if the results are negative, the matter will be dropped; however, if the test is positive, you will be discharged.

Please understand that the intent of the company's proposal is to correct or rehabilitate you. However, failure to elect one of the two options listed above will result in your immediate discharge.

Eight of the employees took drug counseling or tested negative on their retest. One refused to comply with either option and was discharged. The grievant in this case tested positive on a retest on October 24 and was terminated. He later tested negative and was reinstated into a warehouse position, although he had previously been a driver. On March 11, 1985, he was returned to the driver classification.

It was the union's contention that the testing of these employees was not reasonable. The tests showed drug use away from work. As such, the company had to prove that the business or the employee's performance had been prejudiced, which it had failed to do.

The arbitrator, M. Zane Lumbley of Snohomish, Washington, a former National Labor Relations Board field examiner, had to decide whether the employer had the right to require employees to submit to a test. According to Lumbley, the requirements for disciplining an employee for off-duty conduct are that the behavior must harm the company's reputation or product, render the employee unable to perform his or her duties, or lead to refusal, reluctance, or an inability of other employees to work with that employee.

Lumbley sided with the union. Even though the employer had reason to believe that sale and use of drugs and alcohol were occurring during working hours, the test it elected to give could not distinguish where the use had taken place. The test did not determine where or when marijuana had been smoked; it merely indicated that an employee had smoked it at some point within the past thirty days. Since the company was unable to demonstrate any negative effect on its operation because of such off-duty drug use, the workers who had been disciplined were improperly penalized.

This is not to say that employers cannot adopt reasonable rules against drug use to ensure the safety and health of employees. They have a right to protect their employees and to guard against legal liability. Any action taken must, however, be reasonable.

THE DEFINITION OF "OFF DUTY"

An equipment operator at Texas Utilities came off a twelve-hour shift at 7:00 a.m. on October 12, 1982. He met two fellow workers in the company parking lot. After drinking some beer, they drove in the operator's car to an area off company premises called the "clay pits." They spent some time there while the grievant sited his rifle for the squirrel season and the other two employees sat in his car. When they returned to the company parking lot, at approximately 10:00 a.m., they were apprehended by the plant security supervisor and the personnel manager. A marijuana leaf had been found on the bumper of a car parked in the lot. One of the operator's companions, the owner of that car, was asked to open the trunk so that the company could check for more marijuana. He did so and another leaf, resembling marijuana, was found lying on top of various cartons and plastic bags. The owner of the car was asked to remove the contents of the trunk for further search. He refused to do so, saying, "What I've got in my trunk would cause me more trouble than being discharged." He was suspended.

The two company officials then asked to search the operator's car, and he agreed. A partially smoked cigarette, thought to be marijuana, was found in the backseat ashtray. The operator denied having any knowledge of the cigarette. He was then ordered to take a drug test. After discussing the situation and changing his mind several times, the operator resigned, thinking that even if he passed the test, he would still lose his job. Later that day, the plant superintendent received a telephone call from the union steward asking that the resignation be withdrawn, since the employee was now willing to submit to a drug test. The superintendent refused and the union filed a grievance.

A company rule provided, "Where there is reason to believe an employee is under the influence of intoxicants, drugs, or narcotics while on company property, the employee may be required to take a blood test, urinalysis, or other diagnostic tests."

The arbitrator, Samuel Edes, a partner in the Washington, D.C., law firm of Feder and Edes and former deputy undersecretary in the Department of Labor, had to decide whether that rule was properly applied to the facts of this case. He concluded that the ruling turned on whether the grievant was off duty at the time of the incident. He was on company premises, but not as an employee—he was there only to return his two coworkers to their cars. Since his presence was unrelated to his employment, the company representatives could not order him to submit to testing as they could have if they had found him smoking marijuana on the premises and on company time. Nothing about the grievant's behavior indicated that he was under the influence of drugs. This employee was "off duty," although on company premises. The company's request was therefore improper. The grievant was reinstated.

What if the employee had been caught smoking pot in his car in the company lot, outside of working hours? Would an arbitrator reach the same conclusion? What would have happened if the grievant had agreed to take the drug test and it had been positive? Is an off-duty employee, coming to the plant as a visitor, exempt from the work rules? Compare this case with the one that follows.

SMOKING POT IN THE PARKING LOT

In a society that often condones the recreational use of marijuana, it is not surprising that arbitrators encounter many cases involving that drug. Here, the facts were quite simple. The grievant was employed in a retail food store. On November 8, 1980, shortly after 7:00 p.m., he was allowed a half hour for "lunch." He went to his car in the parking lot, planning to leave the premises.

A company security guard walked up to the car. For about fifteen minutes, he and the employee discussed automotive repairs, until the guard noticed the odor of marijuana and demanded that the employee give him the remains of a cigarette that he saw in the ashtray. According to the employee, the cigarette, which was a joint, was left over from the day before. It was quite cold.

The guard escorted the employee to the store manager's office. According to the manager, the employee admitted having smoked marijuana in his automobile. He later denied having made that statement. The manager wrote up discharge papers, based on a company rule stating that the use of drugs during working hours was grounds for termination. The union steward came into the meeting shortly after the discharge. A grievance was filed on November 10.

The employer's position was that the grievant had been terminated for possession and use of marijuana, an illegal drug under Ohio law. His action violated a company rule against use or possession.

The union argued that the evidence failed to show any such use—and certainly not by clear and convincing evidence. Furthermore, the grievant was not on duty when the incident occurred, so the rule was not applicable.

The arbitrator, Professor Timothy J. Heinsz of the University of Missouri, believed the security guard's testimony that the grievant had been smoking marijuana in his car. The guard had no reason to give false testimony. Heinsz also noted that the marijuana use had taken place during the grievant's break. He ruled that such an infraction did not justify termination. Criminal law today regards marijuana use as a minor offense. He also gave weight to the grievant's good work record. Moreover, the rule refers to the use of drugs during working hours. Here, the grievant was on his own time. Based on those considerations, the arbitrator reinstated the grievant, but without back pay.

If the grievant was on his own time when sitting in his car smoking marijuana, then he was not in violation of company rules. Why then did the arbitrator deny him back pay? The result of the award was, in effect, a lengthy suspension—a very stiff penalty.

Labor arbitrators are sometimes criticized for their unwillingness to decide entirely for one side or the other. Reinstatement without back pay is frequently cited as an example. Why should the length of an employee's suspension depend on how long it takes to conclude the arbitration? In this instance, eleven months had passed between the incident and the award—an unusually long period. Who caused the delay? Certainly not the grievant.

In this case, the employee was "off duty" on his lunch break. Nevertheless, he was penalized. In the cases that follow, the employees' activities were even more remote from their work but, for one reason or another, the employers decided that termination was justified. See if you agree.

The case just described is similar to one that is before the Supreme Court of the United States. In *Misco, Inc. v. United Paperworkers International Union*, 768 F.2d 739 (5th Cir. 1985), *cert. granted*, 55 U.S.L.W. 3472 (U.S. 1987), a machine operator was caught in the company parking lot in the back seat of a car that smelled of marijuana. Two other employees were in the front seat, where a joint was burning in an ashtray. The operator denied smoking marijuana. He was terminated, partially because he had a poor work record. Afterward, marijuana was also found in his car and later, pursuant to a search warrant, in his home. The arbitrator, Professor Milden J. Fox of Texas A&M, refused to consider that evidence because the company had fired the grievant before this information came to light. He put him back to work.

A federal district court set aside the award and was upheld by the Fifth Circuit in an opinion that criticized the arbitrator for being "whimsical," "gazing at the trees and being oblivious of the forest," and ignoring "a serious and well-founded public policy." The issue now before the Supreme Court is whether courts must defer to an arbitrator's judgment as long as it draws its essence from the collective bargaining agreement.

The *S.D. Warren* case, described in the introduction of this book, provides an even more obvious example of a court overruling an arbitrator's decision. The *Steelworkers' Trilogy* cases established that such awards should be upheld by the courts where the arbitrator has based the decision on a plausible interpretation of the language of the contract as viewed in light of the bargaining relationship.

DISCHARGED FOR SELLING COCAINE

On February 11, 1982, a drop-hammer operator in the Baltimore plant of Martin Marietta was arrested for selling an eighth of an ounce of cocaine to an undercover detective. The sale took place away from the company's premises. The employee did not notify the company of his arrest, but on February 18, he discussed his drug addiction with the company doctor. He was referred to a treatment program where he underwent counseling.

In March, after discovering that information about his arrest could no longer be kept from the company, the employee told the manager of employee relations about his indictment. A trial date had been set for July. He also admitted using cocaine over the past three years and a prior conviction for possession of marijuana. He disclosed that his absences from work had been due to drug use.

On July 7, the employee pleaded guilty, was convicted, and received a term of ten years, which was suspended subject to his serving five years' probation. He was required to continue rehabilitation and to devote 300 hours to community service.

After reviewing the court records, the company decided to discharge the employee. It relied on a work rule that stated, "Shameful or indecent conduct is prohibited. Conviction for any major offense, regardless of whether or not committed at the company, will be considered inexcusable conduct." This was the first time that Martin Marietta had discharged a worker for a major offense away from company property, although, in some earlier cases, employees had quit or been terminated because of incarceration.

This employee had a lengthy history of drug abuse. He had used cocaine for years, seeking help from his family physician even before going to the company doctor in February. A complete record of his extensive drug-treatment history was presented to the arbitrator. The employee said that he was now cured. The union contended that discharge was too severe in light of the employee's continuing medical treatment. A claim was also made that he was being punished for union activity.

The arbitrator, Louis Aronin, a former deputy director of the Office of Labor Management Relations of the U.S. Civil Service Commission and an adjunct professor at Georgetown Law Center, disagreed with the union's contentions. He based his decision on the fact that the grievant did not seek assistance until after his arrest. In fact, the employer did not learn of the criminal proceedings until after the grievant had been indicted. All of the actions taken by the grievant after his arrest led the arbitrator to believe that they were done "to establish a pattern of conduct which would mitigate any future penalty by the employer." The arbitrator also found that the grievant was not a casual user of cocaine. His use had lasted at least four or five years, and he had also sold drugs. The grievant admitted that drugs had sometimes affected his performance at work. And, finally, he did not turn to the drug-rehabilitation program until after his arrest. Aronin found no basis for mitigation and denied the grievance.

WOULD YOU WANT THIS WOMAN COUNSELING YOUR CHILDREN?

The grievant in this case had been working as a home counselor for the Elyria board of education in Ohio since 1977. In May of 1984, her supervisor learned through a newspaper article that the counselor's husband had been indicted for drug trafficking. The supervisor called her into his office to discuss the situation. The grievant claimed that she had no involvement with illegal activities.

Shortly afterward, the counselor was indicted on seven felony counts. Again, her supervisor learned about it from the local newspaper. She assured him that there was nothing to the charges. The supervisor nevertheless decided that it would be better for her to work in his office than in the field with children or parents. During that period, the grievant was given clerical duties and did not see any students.

On April 3, she was found guilty on one count of the indictment: her premises had been used for a felonious offense. The supervisor once again learned of the even through the news media. He advised her that her future employment would be carefully scrutinized and asked whether she would prefer to quit. She declined to resign.

The counselor had a chance to tell her side of the story at a meeting held with the business manager of the school system on April 15. She was represented by counsel. On the following day, the business manager sent her a letter of termination. It said that her offense was inconsistent with counseling children about their personal problems, including drug abuse. Her union filed a grievance.

The board of education confirmed the termination at its meeting on April 23. The grievant appealed to the Civil Service Commission, which denied her appeal on the ground that the board's action was justified.

In June, the grievant was sentenced to six months in jail. Again, her employer learned about it from the papers.

The issue before the arbitrator, Professor Hyman Cohen of Cleveland State University's College of Law, was whether the off-duty activities of the grievant justified her termination. In general, arbitrators confirm disciplinary actions where an employee's wrongful behavior has harmed the employer. Cohen held that this discharge was for just cause. Her duties were to counsel children and parents, sometimes about drug-related problems. Her conviction was therefore related to her employment. Drugs have a "corrosive impact," especially upon youth. The grievant held a position of trust. She had to be above reproach.

The union had tried to make use of the fact that the incident occurred almost a year before the grievant was discharged, but the arbitrator pointed out that she had been assigned to office work as soon as the school board found out about her indictment. For more than ten months, she had not been performing her regular duties as a home counselor.

Another factor considered by the arbitrator was the publicity given to her indictment, conviction, and sentencing, all of which appeared in the local newspapers, as did the fact that the judge refused to grant her probation. Such notoriety strengthened the school board's case.

SHOULD A DRUG PUSHER WORK WITH THE MENTALLY RETARDED?

The grievant, who worked with patients in a state residence for the retarded, was one of thirty-one persons arrested in a drug raid. The local newspapers printed her name, but did not report where she worked. The charges were for three counts of delivering controlled substances: 2.9 grams of hashish on March 25, 1983; 50 units of Demerol on December 21, 1983; and 46 units of Demerol on February 1, 1984. These were felony counts.

When notified of the situation, her employer, Polk Center of Pennsylvania's Department of Public Welfare, suspended the aide for thirty days and later terminated her. The action was based on unfavorable publicity and a lack of mitigating factors.

The arbitrator, Charles Feigenbaum of Wheaton, Maryland, formerly deputy director of the Office of Labor Management Relations in the U.S. Office of Personnel Management, put her back to work. He felt that the original suspension had been for just cause. At that time, serious charges were pending. It was appropriate that the employer not take any chances. But the employer should then have investigated the case, which it did not do.

The termination was based on the three criminal charges. The employer did not know at that time that the grievant had pleaded guilty to one of them. In any case, criminal activity does not automatically justify discipline; some connection to the job must be shown. According to Feigenbaum, the offenses were not related to the grievant's employment. Here, no adverse publicity about the center was demonstrated, nor was there any indication that the employer's reputation had been jeopardized. It is also important to note that there was never any question of a connection between the grievant and the center's drugs. She had no access to them. Medication was kept under lock and key by the nurses, and there was no indication that drugs were missing. The arbitrator ordered reinstatement with full back pay and benefits.

ARE CORRECTIONAL WORKERS IN A SPECIAL CATEGORY?

The grievant here was employed at a state correctional facility, where she worked as a counselor. Among her responsibilities were administering breathalyzer tests and guiding inmates through the rehabilitation process, making sure that they avoided further substance abuse.

At 3:30 one morning, her automobile was stopped by a deputy sheriff. She was found to be driving under the influence of alcohol. On the breathalyzer test, she registered .195 percent. The police advised her supervisor. The counselor pleaded guilty and received eighteen months' probation. Her supervisor suspended her for one day without pay.

Since the counselor felt that her off-duty conduct should be of no concern to her employer, she asked the union to file a grievance. The issue was whether discipline can be imposed for off-duty activity without the employer demonstrating that it had been adversely affected.

Arbitrator Stanford C. Madden of Kansas City, Missouri, a former attorney with the National Labor Relations Board, found that the grievant's case turned on the fact that she worked in a correctional facility. Ordinarily, an employee's conduct away from work is not a subject of concern. But it is imperative that correctional personnel maintain a good image in order to gain the respect of the inmates. He agreed with the county that "the grievant, as an employee of a law related agency, is bound to a higher standard of conduct than public employees at large because of the nature of her duties." The grievant's conduct could have a negative impact on prisoners undergoing rehabilitation. In this case, the counselor worked closely with inmates. This made her a "role model" whose misconduct could serve as a bad example.

The Polk County Department of Corrections had a rule that required employees to refrain from conduct "incompatible with their employment and to avoid willful violation of the law." The grievant was aware of the rule. With that in mind, the arbitrator agreed that the county's one-day suspension was warranted.

In this case and the two prior ones, employees were disciplined because of their status as trusted counselors of people with problems. That special relationship was, in each case, threatened by their off-duty activities. The next case involves workers in a nuclear power plant. Is there also a reason to hold them to a higher standard of off-duty behavior?

MUST NUCLEAR WORKERS BE DRUG FREE?

Some work environments are so inherently dangerous that they require an employer to impose strict penalties upon workers for alcohol or drug abuse. A nuclear plant, because of its potential danger to the public and the employees, falls into that category.

This case arose at Detroit Edison's Enrico Fermi Energy Center. In April of 1984, just before nuclear fuel was to be brought to the site, the company issued a work rule establishing a hard-line policy on drug abuse: the use of illegal drugs on and off company premises would not be permitted. Random drug tests of employees would be conducted periodically. Employees found to be using drugs would be removed from the site until they were "drug free."

The grievants in this case underwent an immunoassay of their urine administered by an independent laboratory. Samples found to be positive were tested again by another laboratory, using gas chromatography/mass spectrometry. A cut-off point of twenty nanograms was considered drug free.

After both cycles of tests, two employees were found to have traces of THC, the active ingredient of marijuana. They were suspended for three days and placed on paid sick leave until they could be determined to be drug free.

The company justified its policy as being necessary to ensure a safe workplace and to meet the Nuclear Regulatory Commission's requirements for an operating license. The definition of "drug" was established consistent with the Controlled Substances Act of 1970. Only drugs prescribed by a physician were exempt. The goal was to establish a drug-free environment.

The union said that the company's policy went too far. No evidence suggested that the employees were unable to perform their duties in a safe manner. Furthermore, NRC guidelines neither required nor specifically recommended the steps taken by the company. The union also raised constitutional issues.

The question before the chairman of the arbitration panel, Professor Dallas L. Jones of the University of Michigan's School of Business Administration, was whether the drug policy was reasonable. The union and the company each appointed "advisors" who sat with him as arbitrators on the panel.

Jones concluded that the NRC was legitimately concerned about the use of drugs; an employee who works in a nuclear plant should not be a user. It does not matter whether the use occurs on or off duty. The risks of operating a nuclear facility require the highest standards. While arbitrators are reluctant to give employers the right to regulate off-duty conduct, they may do so when there is a reasonable relationship between such conduct and the needs of the employer in the operation of its business.

In deciding that the company's policy of random drug testing was reasonable, the arbitrator employed a balancing test: the individual's constitutional right to privacy was weighed against the deterrent effect that such a policy would have on drug use. The right to privacy is essential, but there are times when it must give way to the public good. The safe operation of a nuclear facility is of the utmost importance to its employees and to the public.

The arbitrator nevertheless ruled that the two grievants should be reinstated, because the company had not given adequate notice of its policy. The publication announcing the policy had been distributed at the plant, but the grievants had testified that they were unaware of it. Absent prior notice of the policy, it was unfair to penalize employees for violating it. The arbitrator's decision put them on notice, however, that future violations would result in disciplinary action.

Jones noted that one expert had testified that there was no connection between the amount of THC metabolites in the urine and the time elapsed since marijuana use. The test readings would therefore be meaningless, varying from day to day. He said that he found nothing in the scientific literature that associated impairment (or inability to work) with the presence of THC metabolites. An employee could be "drug free" even while testing positive for the metabolites. In the future, evidence that the metabolites themselves can have an effect on the central nervous system might become available. At present, the expert testified, there are no scientific data to sustain such a conclusion.

On the basis of this information, Jones found that the company had no right to place employees on paid leaves of absence unless there was evidence of their inability to work in a safe and efficient manner.

MUST A UNION BE GIVEN PRIOR NOTICE?

For many years, the city of Pittsburgh required a physical examination of employees returning from an illness or from an injury after more than fifteen days of absence. In January of 1986, the city decided to add a urine test to that physical, looking for evidence of drug use. The union was not notified in advance.

The two grievants in this case, Pittsburgh firefighters, returned from absences for compensable injuries and were given examinations, including the urine test, which, unknown to them, was for drugs. Both tested positive for exposure to marijuana. They were ordered to undergo a second test and appear before a trial board. One firefighter was fined six days' pay. Local 1 filed a grievance on his behalf.

The case came before arbitrator William J. Hannan, a professor at the University of Pittsburgh. The union complained about the lack of notice. The employees did not know that they would be subject to drug testing. Hannan agreed. The bargaining agreement required the city to give the union at least fifteen days' notice prior to changing any past practice.

As Hannan explained, the purpose of drug testing is not to catch employees, but to warn them that they will be disciplined if found to be users. "Prevention by advance notice of testing is preferred to remedial testing." He ordered that the grievant be reimbursed and any record of the test removed from his file.

What would have been the result if the union had argued that the drug test was unconstitutional? Does the city's right to supervise employees give it the right to impose such a test? What right has the city to require any physical examination unless it demonstrates a connection between the illness or injury and the job responsibilities of the particular employee? Should firefighters be subject to more rigorous screening than other city employees?

SUMMARY

The cases in this chapter demonstrate that drinking or drug abuse occurring away from work will not be justification for job discipline unless they affect the employee's work. Work might be affected in various ways. Either the employee's performance could suffer or drug use could keep the employee away from work. In other cases, drug or alcohol abuse might damage the employee's image, which could be vital to the ability to perform effectively. In still other situations, a job may be so dangerous that the employer can justify imposing stricter prohibitions on drug or alcohol use. The arbitrator must then balance the employer's need for safety or security against the rights of the employees. There are many variations on that theme.

CITATIONS

One Last Chance: Westvaco, U.S. Envelope Division *and* Southern California Printing Specialties and Paper Products Union, District Council No. 2, 319 *Summary of Labor Arbitration Awards* (AAA) 12 (1985).

What Urine Tests Don't Prove: Board of Education of the District of Columbia *and* American Federation of State, County and Municipal Employees, District Council 20, Local 2093, AFL-CIO, *Arbitration in the Schools* (AIS) 193-10 (1986).

A Drug Test for the Night Shift: CFS Continental, Inc. *and* International Brotherhood of Teamsters, Chauffeurs, Warehousemen and Helpers of America, Local 117, 86-1 *Labor Arbitration Awards* (ARB) ¶ 8070 (1986).

The Definition of "Off Duty": Texas Utilities Generating Company *and* International Brotherhood of Electrical Workers, Local 2337, 82 *Labor Arbitration Reports* (LA) 6 (1984).

Smoking Pot in the Parking Lot: Seaway Food Town, Inc. *and* United Food and Commercial Workers International Union, Local 31, 9 *Labor Arbitration Information System* (LAIS) 1015 (1982).

Discharged for Selling Cocaine: Martin Marietta Aerospace, Baltimore Division *and* United Automobile, Aerospace and Agricultural Implement Workers of America, Local 738, 298 AAA 9 (1984).

Would You Want This Woman Counseling Your Children?: Elyria Board of Education *and* Individual Grievant, AIS 194-3 (1986).

Should a Drug Pusher Work with the Mentally Retarded?: Commonwealth of Pennsylvania *and* American Federation of State, County and Municipal Employees, District Council 85, *Labor Arbitration in Government* (LAIG) 3599 (1985).

Are Correctional Workers in a Special Category?: Polk County, Iowa *and* American Federation of State, County and Municipal Employees, Local 1868, 80 LA 639 (1984).

Must Nuclear Workers Be Drug Free?: Detroit Edison Company *and* Utility Workers Union of America, Local 223, AFL-CIO, AAA Case No. 5430-0285-85 (unpublished).

Must a Union Be Given Prior Notice?: City of Pittsburgh *and* Pittsburgh Fire Fighters, Local 1, LAIG 3834 (1987).

CHAPTER 5

The Test of Chronic Abuse

In evaluating drug or alcohol violations, an arbitrator considers the reasonableness of the action taken by an employer and the consistency with which a rule has been enforced. In addition, employers must show that the employee knew or should have known of the rule and was aware or should have been aware that violation could result in discharge. Sufficient notice of a rule can be given by distributing it in written form to all employees, including it in an employee manual, or posting it on signs around the plant. Notice can also be verbal, such as emphasis of the rule at orientation meetings. If the issue of notification is likely to be raised in arbitration, it is helpful to have a written record.

When considering the reasonableness of a work rule relating to drugs and alcohol, an arbitrator may also consider the nature of the industry, the particular hazards created by their use, or the impact of their use on an employer's reputation.

Inconsistent application of substance-abuse rules may prompt an arbitrator to overturn disciplinary action. The obligation to be consistent does not, however, require that every violation be handled in exactly the same manner. Even though a rule might prohibit possession, use, and reporting to work under the influence of drugs or alcohol, possession may be deemed a less-serious offense than actually using the substance in the plant, which might, in turn, be considered less severe than being "under the influence."

In the cases that follow, arbitrators are required to review various managerial decisions about chronic abuse of alcohol and drugs. Which factors impress the arbitrators in these cases? Are the interests of the grievant adequately protected? What do you think?

A CHRONIC ALCOHOLIC

What should be done about a worker who admits to being a chronic alcoholic? At what point is discharge appropriate?

This case involved an employee whose drinking had resulted in excessive absenteeism. He had been suffering from alcoholism for several years. Insurance claim documents and community mental-health evaluations from as far back as 1976 were submitted by the employer as background material at the arbitration hearing.

In 1980, Tecumseh adopted an absence control policy, a system of three steps applied progressively: first came a verbal warning, next a written warning, and then termination. That policy was applied to the employee in 1982. He had forty-one excused absences and seven unexcused. The union objected but, after three written warnings (two more than the policy called for), the employee was given a final warning in 1983. The company demonstrated that the grievant's absences were usually caused by alcoholism.

On December 22, the company scheduled a conference about the employee's illness. He informed the employer by telephone that he would not be able to come to the meeting because of his medical problems. He also failed to show up on January 3. On January 4, he returned to work. A meeting was held that day between management, the union, and the employee. It was determined that the grievant would be suspended pending an investigation, which would continue on the following day.

That evening, the employee telephoned his employer to say that he was ill. The employer urged him to see a physician immediately. The employee was hospitalized for a two-week period and released for duty on January 18. Again, a meeting was held. For the first time, the grievant admitted that alcoholism was the cause of his attendance problems. Tecumseh agreed to continue his employment on the condition that he seek professional treatment by a doctor and enroll in a suitable rehabilitation program. The doctor had to confirm treatment and provide periodic reports on the progress of the employee and certify that he had stopped drinking.

During the ensuing weeks, the employee missed work on February 7 and 8, when he was hospitalized with a virus. On February 10, he had to leave work early. The next day, he was again absent. On February 14, another meeting was held. The grievant was suspended subject to getting a letter from his doctor. Later that day, he called the employer several times. His speech was slurred. A final meeting was held on February 15, after which the employee was terminated. A grievance was filed.

At the arbitration hearing, the company defended its position: enough was enough. Under pressure, it had given the grievant one last chance to live up to his agreement of January 18, a reasonable offer in light of the employee's lengthy history of absence. He had failed that final test.

A representative of Alcoholics Anonymous testified for the grievant at the hearing. She pointed out that denial of alcoholism and dishonesty about one's condition are two symptoms of the disease. Alcoholism is progressive. Treatment does not always lead to recovery. She said that the term "alcohol abuse" is a misnomer. Alcohol was the grievant's problem. Its initial use began a process from which he could not extricate himself. Alcoholics are unable to say whether they will continue to abstain. The answer to that question varies every day with one's desire and motivation.

The arbitrator, Professor John J. Murphy of the University of Cincinnati College of Law, had to decide whether discharge was appropriate, considering the undisputed fact that the grievant was a chronic alcoholic. He expressed sympathy for the grievant's problem but sustained the discharge.

The employer had had ample cause to terminate the employee on several occasions. Instead, it chose to give him second, third, and fourth chances. At various times during the course of the grievant's saga, the company tried to get him to admit that alcoholism was at the root of his problems. Until January 18, he refused to concede this. The company had made considerable efforts to act with fairness.

The arbitrator did not attempt to determine the

earliest stage at which the employer could have discharged the grievant. His finding was that, when the employer offered one final chance on January 18, it was acting reasonably under the circumstances. Accordingly, the discharge was sustained.

As the arbitrator put it, any agreement to abstain that the employee might have made with the company could have become "a trap out of which he could not extricate himself." With chronic alcoholics, employers have to ask themselves, "how far must we go?" In some cases, alcoholism is incompatible with permanent employment.

AN AIRLINE'S APPROACH
TO ALCOHOLISM

An Eastern Airlines flight attendant from Newark was assigned to fly to Atlanta on June 29, 1978. The trip called for a twenty-six hour layover. He went "out on the town," drinking a number of Kahluas. As he later testified, "They go down easy on a summer day."

When he reported for duty at 6:30 that evening, he had to be removed from his flight assignment for being intoxicated. He was sent back to Newark as a passenger. On July 9, the attendant was notified that he was terminated. A grievance was filed on his behalf.

On July 17, he entered a hospital-based alcohol rehabilitation program, from which he discharged himself on July 21, claiming that he was rehabilitated.

The union argued that the grievant had not realized that he was an alcoholic until after he was terminated. He should have been entitled to reinstatement and allowed to enter the company's rehabilitation program.

The arbitrator, the late Burton B. Turkus, a colorful veteran arbitrator from New York City, considered the union's line of reasoning inconsistent with the eligibility provisions of Eastern's program, which offered participation only in the following circumstances: (a) self-referral by the employee prior to any disciplinary action by the company; (b) intervention by a supervisor, coworker, or friends; or (c) company confrontation, for employees whose misconduct is due to alcohol abuse, but where the discipline imposed is less than discharge.

Turkus felt that self-referral to the company's program had come too late. The program was offered to employees either prior to disciplinary action or where discharge was not imposed. This was not a "one free shot" program. The grievant had reported to duty under the influence of alcohol, wholly unfit for work. That was just cause for discharge, particularly since Eastern must maintain a high level of safety if it is to operate an efficient and reliable airline.

A contrary decision was recently upheld in a very similar case, *Northwest Airlines, Inc. v. Air Line Pilots Association, International,* 808 F.2d 76 (D.C. Cir. 1987). The U.S. Court of Appeals, District of Columbia Circuit, had supported a 1982 arbitration decision of a board of adjustment, which held that a pilot who suffered from alcoholism should be offered reinstatement, without back pay, upon proof that he had recovered— including total abstinence from alcohol for not less than two years. The pilot had been drinking during a stopover between flights and, after serving as copilot on the final leg of the trip, showed a blood-alcohol level of .13 percent. After being suspended, he completed the company rehabilitation program and was recertified by the FAA in 1985.

The airline had asked the district court to set aside

the award, which it did on the grounds that it was against public policy. The court of appeals ruled differently. Circuit Judge Harry T. Edwards, formerly a professor of law at the University of Michigan and an active labor arbitrator, pointed out that an arbitration award that draws its essence from the parties' agreement must be enforced, even where a court might disagree on the merits.

Under the Railway Labor Act, which applies to airlines, adjustment board awards are final and binding and may not be set aside except for failure to comply with the law or to confine themselves to matters within the scope of the board's jurisdiction, or for fraud or corruption. In this case, the court of appeals held that the award fell within the scope of the agreement. Termination for just cause is a common issue for arbitrators. The fact that safety was involved did not justify making an exception. As Justice Edwards put it, "It would be the height of judicial chutzpah for us to second-guess the present judgment of the FAA in recertifying [this pilot] for flight duty."

Prohibitions against the use of alcohol by employees of transportation firms are nothing new. When Buffalo Bill Cody was hired to ride for the Pony Express in the early 1880s, he signed an oath of fidelity, swearing "before the Great and Living God, that during my engagement, and while I am an employee, I will, under no circumstances, use profane language, that I will drink no intoxicating liquors, that I will not quarrel or fight with any other employees."

I wonder whether that work rule was honored as often in the breach as such prohibitions are currently. Those riders were an unruly lot, but no more so than some workers today. Technology changes; human nature holds its ground.

ALCOHOLISM ALONE IS
NOT JUST CAUSE

Hercules runs the Radford Army Ammunition Plant in Virginia, making explosives and propellants. The grievant was a maintenance mechanic with seventeen years' seniority. In early 1984, he notified the company that he had an alcohol problem and was admitted to the Waddell Center for treatment. He returned to work on February 20, 1984, but continued to receive counseling for his alcoholism. The company asked him to sign an Infraction of Rules form, which obliged him to "work regularly without evidence of alcohol" and continue to participate in the alcohol counseling program. It also specified that if he failed to comply with any of the conditions, he would be discharged.

On June 10, 1985, the grievant admitted himself to Saint Albans Psychiatric Hospital for further treatment of his alcoholism. Upon his return, he was discharged for failing to comply with the company's requirements. The union filed a grievance.

At an arbitration hearing on April 11, 1986, the union explained that the grievant had asked the company for a week's vacation to enter Saint Albans. He had four weeks' vacation accrued. After entering the hospital, he discovered that his request had been denied. The union also pointed out that the grievant's alcoholism had never affected his work.

The arbitrator, Dr. Lloyd L. Byars, a professor at the Graduate School of Business at the University of Atlanta, agreed with the union. Alcohol dependency usually manifests itself in excessive absenteeism, reduced productivity, or reporting for work under the influence. Here, there was no such evidence. The grievant was asked to sign an Infraction of Rules agreement only because he had sought treatment for his illness. That should not be considered an offense. As the arbitrator explained, "It is not uncommon for an alcoholic to suffer a relapse in his rehabilitation. Many of those who do, however, go on to lead alcohol free lives after additional treatment."

The arbitrator noted that alcoholics employed by contractors and subcontractors of the federal government are protected by the Rehabilitation Act of 1974, which specifies that a defense contractor cannot discharge an employee solely because of alcoholism if it is unrelated to job performance. This is what Hercules was attempting to do here.

The arbitrator upheld this grievance. "A distinction has to be made between alcohol-related absences and absences related to the treatment of alcohol. To hold otherwise would be to punish the very behavior which the company should be encouraging."

Arbitrators recognize that alcoholism is a disease. Where an employee is attempting to salvage a career and is willing to participate in rehabilitation, the arbitrator is likely to offer a second chance.

ONE LAST CHANCE

Companies are often concerned that no matter how terrible an alcoholic's record might be, they may have to continue his or her employment. They fear that termination will not be upheld because the problem will be diagnosed as an illness. The arbitrator will then give the employee chance after chance.

This case involved a grievant who worked as a water hydraulic repairman in the Division of Water and Heat. Almost as soon as he began his job in 1980, he started to accumulate warnings and suspensions. He abused sick leave and was chronically late. He was absent without leave. He even stole gasoline from the city. Time after time, he was suspended and reprimanded and warned. Finally, on April 23, 1985, he was given a five-day suspension for again being AWOL and put on final warning. At that point, the union notified the city that the repairman had "personal" problems. He was referred to a counseling program.

On his first day back from suspension, the employee was late. On the following day, he was absent without leave. He was suspended and then discharged on May 5.

The city pointed out that the grievant had a miserable record and that progressive discipline, tempered with leniency, had been applied. It should not be required to employ someone who was not available for work. The city also testified that it had never been told that the grievant was an alcoholic. It had referred him to counseling for an unspecified "personal" problem.

The union, of course, stressed the alcoholism issue. The counseling program had referred the grievant to Kaiser, a health-care facility. He remained for a week as an inpatient. Diagnosed as an alcoholic, he then joined a halfway house called Fresh Start. He also enrolled in Alcoholics Anonymous. Since being admitted to Kaiser, the union said, the grievant had been sober. Alcoholism, according to the union, is a progressive disease. Only something like the loss of a job makes alcoholics come to grips with their problem. The grievant was now aware of his alcoholism. He should be given another chance.

The arbitrator, Professor Harry E. Graham of Cleveland State University, acknowledged that the grievant had not met even the most minimal requirements of employment. "Standing alone, the alcoholism experienced by the grievant is insufficient to merit return to the employ of the city." But he went on to say that since the grievant now recognized his problem and had "dealt with it in a forthright fashion, the termination should be modified. . . . Where the city has been deficient is in not considering the events subsequent to discharge."

The arbitrator ordered the grievant to be returned to employment. For twelve months, the grievant must furnish evidence of regular attendance at Alcoholics Anonymous. The city could also require proof that the grievant remained sober.

Based on this decision, employers would remain on the hook even after they have terminated an alcoholic for just cause. If rehabilitation occurs, an arbitrator might send the grievant back to work. But not every arbitrator would agree that an alcoholic should be given another chance, despite the fact that the alcoholism may not have been identified until after the termination. In the case that follows, another arbitrator says that only the facts available at the time of the discharge need be considered.

IS ALCOHOLISM A DISEASE LIKE EMPHYSEMA?

Here, again, an alcoholic accumulated a lengthy record of absenteeism that began soon after he was hired in 1977. In 1983, the employer considered discharging the employee. After the grievant entered an alcoholism program, however, he was given another chance, starting the progressive discipline cycle once again.

The situation came to a head in June of 1984, when the employee missed four days' work, returning with a doctor's statement indicating that he had been ill. When the company learned that the employee had not visited the doctor, but had only called him on the telephone complaining of acute anxiety and vomiting, the company decided that enough was enough. He was discharged on July 2, 1984, for excessive absenteeism.

Arbitrator Richard L. Kanner, an attorney from Southfield, Michigan, pointed out that, except for the defense of alcoholism, there would be no question but that this grievant could be terminated. An employer has the right to expect reasonable attendance. The grievant's absences were almost six times higher than average. Kanner noted, however, that alcoholism is acknowledged to be a disease, and that alcoholics are treated much as if their absences had resulted from "diabetes, emphysema or any other such illness."

Kanner spelled out the considerations to be applied in such a case. The employee's absences must result from a particular diagnosed illness, not from other factors. The medical prognosis must indicate recovery within a reasonable time. Just cause must be determined from the facts available to the employer at the point of discharge. Here, the grievant had consistently tried to justify his absences by using excuses such as his car, babysitter, or ex-wife, never mentioning his drinking. Nevertheless, Kanner was convinced that alcoholism was at the root of the problem.

It is difficult to determine whether an alcoholic is likely to recover. In this case, the employer was offered no medical prognosis by the grievant. In fact, he still did not acknowledge his illness. The grievant should have known that he was an alcoholic—certainly after his voluntary treatment in 1983. The employer had no duty to force him to accept further treatment. As the employer stated in its published alcoholism policy, the decision to accept treatment for any suspected illness is "the responsibility of the employee. . . . This is a commonly accepted principle, and alcoholism will not be an exception."

At the point of discharge, the grievant had been excessively absent. In the employer's eyes, the grievant had "an incurable illness resulting in the probability of continued excessive absence. In such a case, the employer is entitled to the reasonable attendance of grievant and, hence, the discharge was based on just cause."

The arbitrator's view was that after the employee had been discharged, a sudden decision to accept treatment for alcoholism would not be allowed to affect the employer's position. By restricting his review to the facts that were available to the company at the time of the discharge, Kanner did not require the employer to give the alcoholic another chance—even a grievant who entered a treatment facility, joined Alcoholics Anonymous, and had not touched alcohol since his discharge.

To that extent, alcoholism is not like emphysema. The alcoholic can stop drinking. The victim of emphysema has no such option.

WOULD YOU TAKE HIM BACK?

In another case involving an employee discharged for excessive absenteeism, arbitrator Marcia Greenbaum from Boston, Massachusetts, later to become president of the Society of Professionals in Dispute Resolution, held that the union had missed the deadline for filing its grievance. In spite of this, she suggested that the company take back the grievant on a conditional basis.

This employee had been disciplined seven times over a two-year period, beginning in 1979, for repeated absences from work. In March of 1982, he was suspended for thirty-one days for reporting to work under the influence of alcohol. The company warned him that this was his last chance. The next time he came in drunk, he would be terminated. His supervisor recommended that he contact the company's employee-assistance program, but the employee thought that he could handle the problem himself. The employee was again suspended in late September for failing to report for work. He admitted that he had been drinking. The supervisor gave him another warning.

On October 4, the employee called to say that he would not be coming to work. The foreman to whom he spoke thought that he had been drinking and told him so. One word led to another and the foreman finally hung up on the employee. In a later call, the employee stated that he was not drunk, but had taken some medication (Tylenol and Alka Seltzer Plus) that made him feel drowsy. The following day, he was discharged. On November 22, he entered a rehabilitation program, which he successfully completed. He met with Alcoholics Anonymous on an after-care basis.

Greenbaum's decision to sustain the discharge was based on the union's late filing of the grievance. The substantive merits of the case were never decided. Nevertheless, in her award she wrote, "The grievant's efforts to redeem himself show a good-faith attempt to rid himself of his drinking problem and become a productive worker." She suggested that the company take a second look at the situation. If the grievant was still on the wagon and attending Alcoholics Anonymous, he might be re-employed on a conditional basis, requiring continued abstinence from alcohol and regular attendance at AA.

The grievant's efforts at rehabilitation did not emerge until after his discharge. But the arbitrator did not feel that this should be dispositive. The grievant, "like many alcoholics, thought he could help himself and did not need outside assistance, but upon realizing the seriousness of his actions, which realization apparently was triggered by his dismissal, did seek outside help."

Labor arbitrators normally restrict themselves to deciding the issues submitted to them by the parties, resisting any temptation to offer gratuitous advice. Arbitrators are not expected to give humanitarian suggestions to the parties. Their role is to decide grievances based upon the facts and their interpretation of the labor contract.

TERMINATING AN ALCOHOLIC IS NEVER EASY

This case involved a small Pennsylvania state agency called the MILRITE (Make Industry and Labor Right in Today's Economy) Council. It had three employees—an executive director, a research analyst, and an administrative assistant. The grievant held the latter position. She became an alcoholic.

During 1981 and 1982, she was a good worker; in 1983, however, she had many unexplained absences and was reprimanded frequently. The executive director pointed out that the office work virtually stopped when she was out. He never knew when she would be absent or for how long. He had encouraged her to seek confidential help from the State Employee Assistance

Program. She nevertheless continued to be absent without advance notice. The director suspended her several times. Finally, on January 5, 1984, he gave her a last warning, coupled with a five-day suspension.

On August 14, the employee came to the director, obviously upset. She said she wanted to leave her job and move away. He gave her the rest of the day off. That afternoon, he received a call from a police officer, who said that the employee had been found lying on the sidewalk. Did she have a drinking problem? The director conceded that she probably did.

On August 17, the employee called to say that she was under treatment at the Susquehanna Valley Center, an institution for alcoholics. On August 31, the executive director visited her there. He said that he planned to discharge her unless she would agree to resign. She signed a letter that he had prepared: "Please accept my resignation . . . effective September 11, 1984."

Afterward, she changed her mind. Her union filed a grievance on her behalf, asking that the letter be rescinded. The union claimed that the grievant's signature was not voluntary. She had been institutionalized, was undergoing therapy, and was under pressure. She was in no condition to make a rational decision.

Arbitrator Charles Feigenbaum of Wheaton, Maryland, formerly deputy director of the Office of Labor Management Relations in the U.S. Office of Personnel Management, concluded that the grievant should be allowed to rescind her letter. He also found that the employer did not have just cause for discharge. Although the procedures normally called for were followed—using progressive discipline and suggesting the State Employee Assistance Program—the final decision was never implemented. He ruled that reinstatement was appropriate because of the possibility of rehabilitation and the grievant's good work record prior to 1983. On the other hand, he found no basis for back pay, warning the grievant that she had come very close to losing her position with the agency.

All of which indicates how difficult it can be to terminate an alcoholic who is willing to seek rehabilitation.

WAS HE PICKLED ON A
SPICED DILL PICKLE?

This grievant worked for fourteen years as an emergency medical technician on an ambulance crew. Members of such teams are responsible for diagnosing injuries, providing first aid, and deciding whether to call for more help or to transport the patient to a hospital. The ambulance service has a rule that any employee who reports to work with alcohol on his or her breath will not be allowed to work.

On October 6, 1984, the technician received an initial work assignment at the Group Health Hospital. A registered nurse on duty noticed that he smelled of alcohol. This was confirmed by another nurse, and the hospital notified the technician's employer. Later, in the ambulance, two other employees and the partner with whom the technician had been working smelled alcohol on the grievant's breath. By this time, he had fallen asleep.

The employer's field supervisor was notified of the hospital's complaint. He spoke to the technician on the telephone. The technician denied having had alcohol on his breath. Nevertheless, he was immediately suspended.

A half hour later, he called back, telling the supervisor that it must have been a hot spiced dill pickle that he had eaten that morning. His wife, who was a patient at another hospital and who saw him that afternoon, said that she had smelled a strong vinegary, pickle odor. Her half-sister and stepmother confirmed that he smelled of pickles. The stepmother added, somewhat maliciously, that he had the same bad breath that she had noticed on other occasions. The supervisor was not convinced. On the following day, the technician was discharged.

His record had been poor for several years. Since January of 1982, he had been disciplined on nine separate occasions, four of which had been alcohol related. In February of 1984, he had been terminated for excessive tardiness. After an earlier grievance was filed, the employer had agreed to reinstate him if he would complete an alcohol-treatment program and stop drinking. He returned to work in April of 1984. By June, he had "fallen off the wagon." He had then been given a written warning that he would be terminated if he committed any further violations. All this preceded the incident in October.

The company contended that progressive discipline had been applied for almost three years. Considerable patience had been expended on this employee. This latest incident was the last straw.

The arbitrator, Alan R. Krebs of Bellevue, Washington, a former administrative law judge and National Labor Relations Board trial examiner, agreed that there was just cause to terminate the grievant. "By the time of the final incident, the grievant was on notice that any additional manifestation of his alcohol problem would lead to his termination." Given the responsibilities of the job, the employer's action was reasonable. The grievant's behavior not only jeopardized the employer's business relationship with one of its major customers but also placed patients at risk.

The union's main argument was that the company failed to prove that the grievant had shown up for work with alcohol on his breath. The arbitrator disagreed. Several witnesses, all of whom were familiar with the odor of alcohol, testified that alcohol was on the grievant's breath. One of the witnesses had detected the odor even before the time of his claimed pickle eating.

Would the company's case have been stronger if it had required a blood-alcohol test? What should the company have done to enforce its earlier agreement that the grievant would enter an alcohol-treatment program and totally abstain from drinking? Is that kind of agreement enforceable?

THE CASE OF THE
DRUNKEN PIG STICKER

Iowa Meat Processing operated a hog-slaughtering plant in Sioux City. The grievant was a utility butcher who worked on the killing floor, where he and other workers used sharp knives to do the slaughtering. On June 21, 1984, he was discharged because of chronic problems with alcohol.

As is often the case, he had a lengthy record of alcohol abuse. The earliest reference to his use of alcohol was a note from a plant nurse on October 28, 1982. She had talked with the doctor who examined him for an injured right hand. The doctor said that unless the patient accepted treatment for his alcoholism, "he will become more accident-prone and a large liability to the company." The nurse reported the conversation to the plant manager.

On January 28, 1983, a supervisor in the plant reported that the employee appeared to be drunk. His breath smelled of liquor. He admitted having had two beers at lunch. Another supervisor warned him that further drunkenness would not be tolerated.

In February of 1983, the grievant injured his arm while working. After surgery, he spent fourteen months recuperating. When he returned to work on May 1, 1984, he was reassigned to the killing floor. At 10:30 a.m., he had a seizure that caused him to fall to the floor and cut his forehead. He suffered convulsions for about five minutes and was taken to a nearby hospital emergency room. The doctor who treated his cut said that he could return to work on the following day. When he reported for duty, he was sent to the company doctor for an evaluation of his condition and instructed not to return to work until the evaluation was completed.

The doctor's report stated that the employee had liver damage. Since he smelled of alcohol, the doctor advised the employee to seek treatment for alcoholism. The employee became enraged and left the clinic, threatening to see his attorney. The doctor told the company that there was a chance that the seizures would recur unless the employee sought treatment. He also reminded management of his evaluation in 1982 of the employee's condition. The man had a long history of alcoholism and had suffered several times from delirium tremens.

On May 14, the employee came to the plant but was told that he would not be allowed to work until his medical problems were resolved. He again smelled of alcohol. On May 16, at a meeting with management and the union, he was notified that, based on the doctor's opinion, he would have to seek treatment for the seizures before he would be allowed back to work. The employee denied that his problem was caused by alcohol. He attributed the attacks to "ill-fitting dentures" that made it difficult for him to breathe. The employee was assured that treatment for alcoholism would be covered by the company's health-insurance program. He could be placed on a leave of absence while hospitalized. He refused.

Because the employer would not permit the employee to return to work, the union filed a grievance after the meeting, saying that refusal to allow him to work was the equivalent of an indefinite suspension without pay. Another joint meeting was held on June 15. The company made the same offer, but the grievant walked out, refusing to accept treatment. On June 21, the company discharged the grievant for failing to seek help for his diagnosed alcohol problem.

The issue before the arbitrator, attorney Thomas P. Gallagher of Minneapolis, was whether the grievant, because of the possibility of future seizures, presented a hazard to himself and other coworkers, providing justification for his termination. Gallagher ruled that the company had just cause to suspend the grievant, but that the subsequent discharge was inappropriate.

> The grievant should retain the option of seeking treatment, of recovering from his alcoholism and thus of eliminating the cause of his incompetence until, in this proceeding, he is given a final resolution of his disagreement with the employer about the cause of his seizure. With the award in this case, that issue was resolved, and the grievant should be given a reasonable time hereafter to eliminate his incompetence by removing the risk of future seizures.

How far must an employer go for one of its employees? The prevailing view of arbitrators is that management has the responsibility to take corrective action when an employee has a disability which endangers his or her life and those of others. In this case, medical evidence clearly demonstrated that the grievant suffered from severe alcoholism. When the company told the grievant to get help, he continued to deny his alcoholism. The company decided that there was no way to deal with this employee short of discharge.

Gallagher upheld the grievance but continued the suspension until such time as the grievant accepted treatment and abstained from alcohol. If that did not occur within six months of the date of the award, the employer would be free of any obligation to reinstate the employee. The arbitrator also encouraged the employer to investigate whether the grievant could be transferred to a job with no risk of injury. This might be done, he said, without the preconditions of treatment and abstinence. Ordering such a remedy, however, was beyond the arbitrator's authority.

This kind of "one more chance" award in cases of alcoholism is fairly common. Unfortunately, only a few confirmed alcoholics meet the conditions for reinstatement and go back to work. Usually, they merely allow the option to lapse.

WHO CAN BE SALVAGED?

Another example of alcoholism involved a 27-year-old nursing attendant who went to work for the Youngstown Hospital Association right out of high school. He worked for more than seven years with a good record of job performance, but excessive absenteeism and tardiness—common signs of alcohol abuse. This employee had been reprimanded or suspended on fifteen prior occasions, but his absenteeism continued. After his third five-day suspension, he was discharged on January 26, 1983. Only then did he voluntarily accept treatment for alcoholism at a clinic in Youngstown. He was released on February 14, detoxified and ready to return to work. In the meantime, a grievance had been filed by his union.

The union pointed out that alcoholism was an illness. The grievant should be given a second chance. The hospital argued that he had been given many prior opportunities to correct his absenteeism.

The arbitrator, Charles R. Miller of Cleveland, Ohio, a former labor attorney, had to decide whether the employer had just cause to discharge the grievant, based on the information available to it at the time. An additional item to be decided was whether the grievant should be given another chance, since the poor attendance was caused by alcoholism. There was no dispute about excessive absenteeism. This employee had been absent as often as he had been working. At no time had the grievant disclosed his problem with alcohol. He had instead used a variety of other excuses to explain his absences.

In deciding such grievances, arbitrators consider length of service, the character of the employee's past service, and the nature of the offense. They then try to judge the employee's future prospects.

Miller felt that the hospital had constructive notice of the grievant's alcoholism. A head nurse had discussed the problem with the grievant, but he had denied being an alcoholic. Other employees at the hospital with alcohol problems had been given second chances.

The arbitrator pointed out that alcohol dependency is a special problem. "Current therapy focuses on attempts to arrest the disease and restore the person to a useful and respected role in society." The employer realized that alcoholism deserves special treatment and would probably have acted differently if it had known conclusively that the grievant was an alcoholic.

The arbitrator concluded that termination was too

severe a penalty, considering the grievant's disease. The purpose of discipline is to correct faults in behavior and to prevent further infractions. He quoted the hospital's own rules: "The purpose of discipline is always corrective, and except in cases of serious misconduct, the objective will be to enforce discipline that will allow an employee to correct his or her behavior."

Since the grievant now recognized his alcohol dependency and had taken steps to control it, he should be reinstated on a conditional basis, to be agreed upon by the hospital and the union. According to Miller, the evidence did "not compel the conclusion that the grievant is not salvageable and cannot be expected to perform well or on a regular basis for the hospital." On the other hand, he warned the union that the hospital could not be expected to allow further absenteeism.

THERE MUST COME A TIME . . .

They exist in every line of work—the chronic alcoholics—and by their absenteeism shall you know them. How far must an employer go for the alcoholic who is chronically absent? How many warnings? How many counseling sessions? How many hospitalizations?

This case involved a dough mixer who had worked with a bakery in Bluefield, West Virginia, since 1966. He was represented by the teamsters. His problems with alcohol dated back to 1973. In 1974, he was discharged, but was rehired after thirty days in a treatment center. In 1975, he was again hospitalized for alcoholism but, after his release, the attendance problems continued.

In 1983, a new production manager joined the company. Noticing the mixer's poor attendance record, he warned him about his drinking and its possible consequences. The employee continued to miss work during late 1983 and January of 1984. Then, for a time, his attendance improved; this was short-lived, however, and in June his absences again increased. The production manager finally called him at home. When the mixer said that he was sick, the manager told him to see the company doctor. The employee refused and became abusive.

After several calls, the employee saw a company doctor, who returned him to work but referred him to a private physician for his drinking problem. The mixer saw that doctor, but soon began to drink again. The company's personnel manager arranged for the grievant to go once more to a hospital for treatment. Afterward, he received additional counseling for his alcoholism. In July, he was released for work.

For an entire year, the employee maintained a good attendance record. Then, following a week's vacation in July of 1985, he missed twelve days of work while being treated in another rehabilitation center. On July 29, after a meeting with the employee and his shop steward, the company gave him a final warning. He would be fired if there was any further absenteeism.

He missed a week's work in September because of drinking. The company scheduled a meeting to discuss the situation. On the day of the meeting, the grievant called to say that he had been drinking and could not come in. He said that he could not stop drinking. The personnel manager told him to come in when he was sober. On September 17, a final meeting was held, and the employee was discharged. The union then filed a grievance.

At the arbitration hearing on May 1, 1986, the company described its efforts to counsel the grievant and its leniency in giving him time off for treatment. It

seemed clear that, despite numerous attempts at rehabilitation, the grievant could not overcome his problem.
The union, on the other hand, contended that the grievant was cured, demonstrating active participation in
a rehabilitation center and attendance at church and
at Alcoholics Anonymous meetings.

The arbitrator, Carl F. Stoltenberg of Pittsburgh,
who apprenticed with Charles L. Mullin after serving
as a field representative with the state education association, supported the company. Employers cannot be
expected to tolerate chronic absenteeism year after
year. Here, the company had acted compassionately,
providing countless opportunities for rehabilitation.
The grievant had been given a final warning in the
presence of his steward. After this warning, he was
"again drunk and AWOL" due to alcoholism. Discharge was for just cause. The company had more than
met its moral obligation. The grievance was therefore
denied.

The pattern here is typical of chronic alcoholism.
After numerous absences caused by heavy drinking,
a series of counseling sessions and a warning result in
temporarily better attendance. All too often, the problem then recurs. Where is the employer allowed to draw
the line? Obviously, arbitrators will differ on this issue
depending upon their perceptions of the grievant and
their estimates of whether an alcoholic can be salvaged.

A CASE FOR REHABILITATION

Companies that offer grievants the opportunity for
drug rehabilitation may find that arbitrators will require them to stand by that offer.

The case at the Weyerhaeuser Company, a wood-product manufacturer in the Northwest, involved a raw-material inspector. On April 18, 1985, the employee came to work at about 7:00 a.m. According to the plant superintendent, he was "sweating and nervous and incoherent, and his eyes were dilated." Two other management representatives commented that the worker "did not look right." The superintendent, who confronted him later that afternoon, asked him to submit to a drug test. The employee refused. He explained to the superintendent that after returning home from the plant the night before, he had smoked marijuana and drunk beer. "I partied last night. I'll show positive. I'm not lily white."

The following morning, the superintendent again met with the employee. They discussed the possibility of a rehabilitation program as an alternative to discharge. The employee enrolled in an outpatient program at Kaiser Health, where he had medical coverage. The program included orientation meetings, lectures, scheduled appointments with physicians and counselors, and group meetings.

On April 22, the employee attended a meeting with union representatives and management officials. He had scheduled two sessions with Kaiser—on May 15 and 16, three weeks from the date of the incident—and he presented the appointment slips. According to the grievant, the plant superintendent threw the slips on the floor, insisting that the employee needed detoxification.

When the employee explained to his counselor at Kaiser that the program was unacceptable to his employer, she called the superintendent to discuss the situation. The counselor emphasized that there was no other program and said that the employee had seemed genuinely concerned. She also explained that detoxification was not necessary in this case.

On May 10, after a further meeting with the union, management decided that it had grounds to terminate the worker. The company rule was unusually broad, in that it covered off-duty drug use: "Possessing, dispensing or using a narcotic, barbiturate, mood ameliorating, tranquilizing or hallucinogenic drug, either on duty or off duty, except in accordance with medical authorization is prohibited." A violation was listed as justifying immediate discharge. The union filed a grievance.

During the period between April 18 and May 10, the company charged that the grievant had not attended sessions at Kaiser. The company's position was that it had offered to reinstate the grievant if he entered a full-time rehabilitation program. He had rejected that option when he failed to enter a "suitable" program.

The arbitrator, William Levin, an attorney from North Hollywood, California, expressed sympathy for the grievant, who had attempted to respond to management's demands. "The grievant did take the required steps in terms of rehabilitation. He did go to Kaiser, where he had medical insurance coverage for treatment. He did see a counselor that first day, at least based on Kaiser's records. He did arrange for appointments at the earliest date given him. He did have the counselor call his employer."

Levin conceded that the grievant's drug problem might be too serious to be dealt with at Kaiser. But once Weyerhaeuser agreed to rehabilitation without spelling out the exact parameters of the plan, it was obliged to permit the grievant to complete the program he selected. When it received a written report, it could then make a judgment as to whether the grievant should be terminated.

The arbitrator's decision to reinstate the employee in this case does not mean that employers must offer rehabilitation in all cases of drug abuse, but that when Weyerhaeuser offered the opportunity to enter a rehabilitation program, it had to allow the worker to "play out the string." In hindsight, Weyerhaeuser might have been wise to specify what kind of rehabilitation would be required, perhaps recommending a specific program. But this employee was left to his own devices to look for help.

WHEN DOES ABSENTEEISM BECOME A DRUG PROBLEM?

Is a company obliged to investigate the reasons for an employee's absenteeism before taking disciplinary action?

A bus operator was discharged by the transit district in Alameda–Contra Coasta on August 1, 1984, for repeated absences over an extended period that dated back to December of 1983. The driver's record indicated that she had failed to come to work on almost half of her scheduled days. Under the employer's progressive discipline program, she received numerous notifications, five-day suspensions, and a final warning. The employer concluded that the driver was incorrigible, and she was terminated. Afterward, she revealed that her absences had been caused by a drug problem that she felt was now under control.

The union did not dispute the facts of the case; rather, it claimed that the company's failure to recognize the employee's need for rehabilitation undermined the corrective function of progressive discipline. Since the grievant had now overcome her severe drug problem, she should be returned to work, at least on a conditional basis.

This is one of only a few cases in this book that were heard by panels of three arbitrators, two of whom were appointed by the parties. That system is gradually dying out because it is generally slower, more expensive, and often results in split decisions. The impartial chairperson, David A. Concepcion of Berkeley, California, former associate dean of Hastings Law School, said that the employer had no obligation to investigate the reasons for the grievant's problems. It is up to employees to explain their absences. Then, an employer can decide whether or not corrective discipline is appropriate, after which the employer's action can be contested in a grievance.

The arbitrators' award described the meetings between the grievant and management during the final months of her employment. The record showed that the district did make an effort to help the driver by directing her to a drug-rehabilitation service while corrective discipline was being applied. She did not complete any of the recommended rehabilitation programs, although she did register for some. Her failure to accept the services offered—waiting until after discharge before undergoing rehabilitation—is a case of "too little, too late."

Based on the employer's application of its progressive discipline policy, the entire panel held that there was just cause for discharge. The assumption, Concepcion explained, is that employees accept the responsibility for coming to work on a regular basis. If that becomes impossible, the burden of justifying any absences shifts to the employee.

SUMMARY

Many of the cases in this chapter dealt with alcoholism, often associated with chronic absenteeism. When can the employer say "enough is enough"? Must an attempt be made to salvage an employee who has become an alcoholic?

This is a complex subject. Only glimpses of the psychological and social problems of addiction are visible here. There is little consensus about how to treat an alcoholic or a confirmed drug user. Alcoholism and drug abuse are diseases, but they are also social problems. Alcohol abuse is not entirely a medical problem, nor is it merely a question of morality or strength of character.

A recent article by Fern Asma in the *Employee Benefit Plan Review* reports that alcoholism affects ten percent of all workers, that the propensity toward alcoholism is an inherited trait, and that it can be fatal. An intelligent drug policy, therefore, will require input from the medical, legal, safety, and personnel departments and from the union. Asma recommends that employers document employee behavior. Usually, that will show poor work habits, sickness, or accidents, all related to the employee's job function.

Every alcohol and drug abuse program should include counseling for the employee and, perhaps, for the family as well. Participation in self-help groups such as Alcoholics Anonymous should be encouraged. Follow-up could be required for several years.

The key question in employee relations remains: How many times must an employer rehabilitate an abuser? Asma believes that twice is sufficient. Even then, disciplinary measures such as suspension can be used to motivate the employee.

Alcoholism affects both the workplace and the community. Many of the drivers picked up by police for driving under the influence are alcoholics. In 1985, according to statistics of the National Highway Traffic Safety Administration, thirty-eight percent of those drivers had a blood-alcohol level of .10 percent or more. Some were social drinkers who happened to overindulge, but many were alcoholics who represent continuing threats to society. Alcoholics also tend to be dangerous in their homes. They are often violent, responsible for many accidents that bring harm to themselves and others.

In the workplace, alcoholics come into contact with people who are in a position to intervene. Often, an alcoholic's employer is best situated to see the symptoms of the disease and to bring pressure upon the alcoholic to accept treatment. That is what some arbitrations over alcohol abuse are really about. The union thinks that the employer has not done enough to force the employee into treatment.

Some companies are tempted to overlook alcoholism, saying to the employee, "Show up on schedule. Do your job. Or take the consequences." Progressive discipline is used, leading to termination. Other employers are prepared to treat alcoholism as a medical problem, encouraging workers to accept treatment or to join Alcoholics Anonymous, and using the threat of discipline as a motivating force. The employer's work rules provide an opportunity to intervene.

The alcoholic's fellow employees might prefer to rid themselves of the danger that such a worker poses for them. In addition, an unreliable person on the production line makes more work for others. Alcoholics are not popular at work. Often, employees who see the problems cannot understand why management is not taking more severe action. If the question were submitted for peer review, the alcoholic might be terminated sooner.

Considering the cases in this chapter, ask yourself whether the arbitrators gave enough consideration to the grievant's fellow employees and their right to a safe and productive working environment. Is it fair to allow a confirmed alcoholic to work in the plant?

These cases leave us wondering what ultimately happened to these ill employees. Did those who were given one last chance use it wisely? Did those whose terminations were confirmed find other jobs? Are they still working? Are they institutionalized? Or are they dead?

CITATIONS

A Chronic Alcoholic: Tecumseh Products Company, Somerset Compressor Division *and* International Brotherhood of Electrical Workers, Local 2360, 11 *Labor Arbitration Information System* (LAIS) 1064 (1984).

An Airline's Approach to Alcoholism: Eastern Airlines, Inc. *and* Eastern Airlines Steward and Stewardesses Association, Local 553, 74 *Labor Arbitration Reports* (LA) 316 (1980).

Alcoholism Alone Is Not Just Cause: Hercules, Inc. *and* Oil, Chemical and Atomic Workers International Union, Local 3-495, 332 *Summary of Labor Arbitration Awards* (AAA) 1 (1986).

One Last Chance: City of Cleveland *and* American Federation of State, County and Municipal Employees, Ohio Council 8, Local 100, *Labor Arbitration in Government* (LAIG) 3747 (1986).

Is Alcoholism a Disease Like Emphysema?: Westinghouse Electric Corporation *and* United Brotherhood of Carpenters and Joiners of America, Local 1615, 323 AAA 1 (1986).

Would You Take Him Back?: Boise Cascade Corporation *and* United Paperworkers International Union, Local 900, AAA Case No. 1130-0068-83 (unpublished).

Terminating an Alcoholic Is Never Easy: Commonwealth of Pennsylvania *and* American Federation of State, County and Municipal Employees, Council 90, LAIG 3575 (1985).

Was He Pickled on a Spiced Dill Pickle?: Shepard Ambulance, Inc. *and* International Brotherhood of Teamsters, Chauffeurs, Warehousemen and Helpers of America, Local 763, 85-2 *Labor Arbitration Awards* (ARB) ¶ 8336 (1985).

The Case of the Drunken Pig Sticker: Iowa Meat Processing Company *and* United Food and Commercial Workers International Union, Local 1142, 13 LAIS 1006 (1986).

Who Can Be Salvaged?: Youngstown Hospital Association *and* Service Employees International Union, Local 627, 82 LA 31 (1984).

There Must Come a Time . . . : West Virginia Baking Company *and* International Brotherhood of Teamsters, Chauffeurs, Warehousemen and Helpers of America, Local 175, 334 AAA 2 (1987).

A Case for Rehabilitation: Weyerhaeuser Company *and* Graphic Communications Union, 86 LA 182 (1986).

When Does Absenteeism Become a Drug Problem?: Alameda–Contra Coasta Transit District *and* Amalgamated Transit Union, Local 192, 316 AAA 3 (1985).

CHAPTER 6

The Use of Undercover Agents

Why do employers use undercover agents? They take a risk when they send spies into the workplace. When such agents are exposed, as they eventually are, some degree of trust between workers and management is lost—an important element of sound labor relations.

How about relationships with the union? An employer that uses an agent in a covert drug operation might not want to warn its union in advance. Like any democratic institution, unions have information leaks. In whom can a company confide? A union president might have to share the information with other union officials. Would any union leader feel comfortable keeping such a secret from the membership?

In most cases, information about covert operations must be compartmentalized, even within a management group. How do supervisors feel when they learn that a drug agent has been watching them without their knowledge? Didn't the company trust them?

In many situations, employers are persuaded to use an undercover agent by the local police or some outside investigator. The agent may be a police officer from a local narcotics squad or an employee of a security agency. The agent is assigned to some unskilled position, posing as a new employee, but his or her real purpose is to discover employees who are selling or using drugs. This entails making "friendships," doing deals, buying drugs, and, in due course, reporting offenders to the investigating agency and to management. It is a dirty business and a hazardous assignment.

As the cases in this chapter show, arbitrators must decide whether to trust an undercover agent. Evidence presented by such agents must usually be confirmed by other witnesses, frequently police officers or management.

Successfully placing an undercover drug agent in an industrial plant is not an easy task. It should be approached with extreme caution.

IS IT SMART TO SEND IN THE NARCS?

Lockheed Corporation had a plant in Burbank, California, where drug and alcohol consumption was flagrant, particularly in the parking lot during the lunch break. What to do? There was a company rule prohibiting "reporting to work under the influence of an intoxicating liquor or dangerous narcotic, or consuming an intoxicating liquor or narcotic on company time or property." The company wanted to enforce that rule and requested help from the Burbank Police Department and the Los Angeles County Sheriff's

Department. Undercover operatives from those two agencies came into the plant, posing as workers. Soon, the agents confirmed that many employees were smoking marijuana and drinking, in and around the company parking lot.

The next step for Lockheed was to conduct a drug bust. On September 14, 1979, more than seventy deputy sheriffs and police officers—some in plain clothes, others in uniform—arrested about fifty employees for drug-related offenses. Some workers were held at gunpoint and handcuffed, many spending one to five days in jail. Company security personnel confiscated the employees' badges and told them that they were suspended.

The grievants in this case were charged with marijuana violations. They were terminated from employment on September 26 for either smoking or being in possession of marijuana on company property. The criminal charges against them were later dismissed.

At the arbitration hearing, a union spokesperson was asked whether the union condoned smoking pot inside the plant. "No," was the answer. Do you think that people should be fired who smoke pot inside the plant? "We would expect them to be fired." How about bringing in marijuana? Should they be fired for that? "Yes. If they brought it in knowingly."

At the arbitration, the union introduced as an expert witness a research psychopharmacologist who testified that social, recreational doses of marijuana actually make for a "slightly improved, more satisfied worker," since "boring tasks . . . are made less boring and more interesting under the modest and mild use of marijuana." The company, on the other hand, tried to show that "marijuana usage can and does affect job performance . . . impairing psychomotor capabilities and response time."

The arbitrator, Professor Walter N. Kaufman of the

University of Southern California, pointed out that, under ordinary circumstances, the company's rule would be sufficient to justify discipline for anyone caught drinking or using drugs. But the union had shown that no employee had ever before been terminated for smoking marijuana or drinking at lunch time on company premises. The widespread drinking and smoking of marijuana witnessed by the police officers supported the conclusion that the grievants did not expect to be disciplined, let alone discharged, for using drugs during their lunch break. The employees apparently thought that the parking lots were not covered by the company rule, at least during lunch periods. Consequently, enforcement of the rule had not been anticipated by the employees.

The arbitrator ruled that, after a long period of inaction in the face of open violations of the rule, Lockheed had no right to suddenly begin to enforce such discipline. Advance warning was required so that employees would know that the company intended to enforce the rule in the future. Since no such warning had been given, the grievants were to be reinstated without back pay. Kaufman went on to say that all employees were now on notice that future violations of the company rule against smoking marijuana in the parking lot could lead to discharge.

On the disparity of treatment between marijuana and alcohol: "The day may come when employee offenses involving the use of soft drugs will be commonly handled like offenses involving the use of alcohol. But, at present, it is clear that there is no statutory presumption or other rule of thumb for determining the extent to which an employee is under the influence of marijuana." Lockheed was not required to be in the vanguard of public opinion. It had the right to prohibit any use of marijuana by its employees during the workday.

Kaufman noted that after the bust, large signs were posted in the lot warning against drinking alcohol. That was done because no employees had been disciplined for drinking and, as Lockheed explained, "We were concerned . . . that . . . employees might have gotten the wrong impression." In fact, Lockheed seemed more concerned about marijuana than alcohol.

Was Lockheed well served by embarking on an undercover operation? Kaufman's opinion does not give much guidance on that question, but one can imagine how employees who were accustomed to having an occasional beer or joint during their lunch break felt when crowds of police officers suddenly materialized, rounding up fifty employees and carting them off to the Burbank jail. After that kind of treatment, what kind of loyalty toward Lockheed would remain? What happened to employee morale? Is this enlightened employee relations?

CAVEAT VENDOR

This case involves another company that became concerned about drug use, went to the local police, and was persuaded to employ an undercover informant.

Two employees were arrested as a result of the subsequent investigation. They had offered to sell "speed" to the agent and had actually delivered it. There were two transactions during April of 1981, one for $180, another for $150. The agent was actually sold diet pills by one of the employees; the other supplied caffeine capsules. Both were arrested under an Illinois statute that forbids the "delivery of a purported controlled substance." The criminal charges were later dismissed for lack of "probable cause."

The employees were fired soon after the incident.

Their union filed a grievance. A disagreement arose at the arbitration regarding the meaning of the term "speed," as used in the discussions between the grievants and the undercover agent. The union claimed that the term was used in its generic sense to include such stimulants as diet pills and caffeine. The company, on the other hand, argued that, when referring to "speed," the grievants intended the more common pharmacological definition, a mind-altering substance containing amphetamine.

The arbitrator, Professor Martin A. Cohen of the Illinois Institute of Technology in Chicago, pointed out that the capsules were sold at prices far beyond their retail value. The use of the term "speed" was not accidental.

The union's primary argument was one often made when a criminal action precedes arbitration—that the court's dismissal of the violations against the grievants should be dispositive. Cohen disagreed. An arbitrator need not be governed by what happens in a criminal action. The issues are different, and the forums are independent. "The arbitrator derives authority from the parties' agreement and has the responsibility of deciding whether the company had 'just cause' to discharge the grievants based upon the evidence presented to the arbitrator during the arbitration hearing."

After hearing the evidence, Cohen determined that the grievants' conduct contributed to the plant's drug-trafficking problems by defrauding customers into believing that they were buying an illegal drug. Even though the company had no specific rules outlawing such conduct, the arbitrator felt the behavior was unacceptable. The employees should have been aware that they were risking severe discipline. Both of the grievants were relatively short-term employees with prior disciplinary records. There was nothing in their files to justify mitigation. On that basis, their grievances were denied and the discharges confirmed.

FIRED FOR FLOGGING
TWO BLACK MOLLIES ON CAMPUS

A maintenance-department worker at the State University of New York at Buffalo was fired for selling two amphetamine capsules, commonly known as "black mollies," to an undercover agent. The sale was made on campus, inside the student union.

The agent testified that in July of 1978, the maintenance worker was introduced to him as someone who could get him drugs. The agent indicated his interest. After they met, the agent and the employee became "friends," seeing each other several times a week.

During October of 1978, the agent made arrangements to make a purchase. The two agreed to meet at Grover Cleveland Hall, where the employee worked. The agent arranged to have police officers from a narcotics squad nearby for surveillance and protection. Two detectives were assigned. At about 5:00 p.m. on October 20, the agent went to the designated place but could not find the maintenance worker. He went to look for him at his home, then returned to the student center. He spotted the employee there, having a beer. The agent ordered one for himself. He then asked the price of the pills. The employee responded "$1.50 a hit" and showed the agent two black capsules. The agent complained about the price but gave the employee $3.00 for the capsules.

On the way out, the agent gave the capsules to detectives. They were tested and found to contain amphetamine, a controlled substance. The maintenance worker was subsequently arrested and incarcerated for three weeks. He was also suspended by the university, subject to termination. The criminal trial was pending at the time of the arbitration.

The union argued that, even if the grievant were guilty, discharge was too severe a penalty. Under the labor agreement in this case, no employee could be discharged without an arbitrator's approval. This is unusual. An employee is usually terminated first, and the arbitration is held later.

The arbitrator, William A. Babiskin, an attorney from Albany, New York, and formerly a lawyer for the city of New York, explained that arbitrators use a common approach when deciding the severity of the penalty in cases such as this. He listed seven factors: "whether possession or sale is involved; the type of drug (marijuana or hard drugs); whether the transaction was a casual sale; whether the conduct occurred on the premises of the employer; presence of a drug problem in the workplace; impact on the reputation of the employer; and effect on the orderly operation of the employer's business." Applying those factors to this case, the arbitrator found that the discharge was appropriate.

The grievant was involved in the sale of hard drugs. The record suggests that this was not a casual sale but part of a continuous business venture. Indeed, the grievant tried to get the agent to buy more drugs at a lower price. The sale took place on university property.

> I cannot ignore the special responsibility the State University has to its students and their parents. The State is obligated to see that its campuses are not sanctuaries for the drug trade. It is no secret that drugs are a serious problem on the nation's campuses and this one, in particular. . . . Allowing the grievant's return to duty would have a negative impact on the orderly operation of the University. It would send the wrong message to

the rest of its employees. Dope peddling cannot be condoned or tolerated. Those who traffic in drugs for profit at the workplace do so at their peril. If caught, they face almost certain discharge.

The arbitrator found that the suspension without pay was for good cause. He further held that the proposed penalty—termination—was appropriate.

A VIDEOTAPED POT PARTY
IN THE LOCKER ROOM

This case involved an undercover agent working for a hospital who videotaped a pot party in the men's locker room. Having been hired to investigate problems of theft, the agent became aware that drugs were being used by the custodial staff. A videocamera was installed behind an exit sign in the men's locker room. A microphone was hidden in the ceiling.

On June 1, 1984, at 7:00 a.m., the equipment recorded seven employees, including the grievant, passing around and smoking a hand-rolled cigarette. The grievant was shown rolling and smoking a cigarette of his own. The tapes showed another employee burning an incense stick.

The investigator reported his findings to management. After watching the tape, the executives agreed that the employees were smoking pot. They confronted the workers. The grievant denied having smoked marijuana but received a three-day suspension, followed by termination. He had been a custodian at the hospital since 1980 but had a poor attendance record.

The custodian and five other employees filed grievances. Two of them claimed that they knew about the camera and had acted out the incident to play a trick on the employer. The grievant denied participating in any such hoax. He said that he had been smoking a hand-rolled tobacco cigarette, as had been his custom in recent years. He did admit to off-duty use of marijuana.

The union said that the arbitrator should require proof "beyond reasonable doubt" or, at least, "clear and convincing evidence." By either standard, it contended, the employer fell short. There was no evidence that the substance being smoked was marijuana. The investigator did not collect any of the discarded remains. Nor did the hospital search the employees' lockers.

Nevertheless, the arbitrator, Jonas B. Katz, a lawyer from Cincinnati and a former National Labor Relations Board field examiner, upheld the termination. In his opinion, the evidence established the grievant's guilt. The primary proof was the tapes. The arbitrator had watched them. He became convinced that the seven employees involved were smoking marijuana. The investigator had described to him how people smoke marijuana, and that was how the employees had smoked their cigarettes. Katz conceded that there was no direct evidence that what was being smoked was marijuana, but, based on the circumstantial evidence submitted, he denied the grievance. The hospital rules clearly stated that the use of drugs would result in discharge.

IF YOU MUST DO IT, DO IT RIGHT!

The Abex Corporation employed an undercover agent for over six months, during which time he worked on rotating shifts and in different departments of the plant. In the course of his investigation, the agent made numerous purchases of marijuana from three different employees. These transactions were reported to the investigative agency and then to the employer. The possession or sale of drugs on company property was strictly forbidden. Based on the written reports received from the agency, the company discharged the three employees on August 10, 1981, for selling and using marijuana in violation of company rules. Local 1991 filed grievances.

The union argued that the case should not be based only on the word of the undercover agent who had testified as to the alleged sales of marijuana. In the absence of any corroboration, the union contended that the company had failed to sustain its burden of proof.

The arbitrator, Charles F. Ipavec, an attorney from Cleveland, Ohio, disagreed. The evidence presented by the company was not based solely on the testimony of the agent. It was verified by written reports to the investigative agency, which were introduced at the hearing. In addition, the city's police department had confirmed that the substance involved was marijuana. Therefore, in light of the serious nature of the wrongdoing by the grievants and their poor work records, "discharge is an appropriate penalty even as to the first offense."

This case provides a textbook demonstration of how to use an outside investigative agency to conduct a covert operation. In spite of the union's arguments that the company's action was based on uncorroborated testimony from a questionable source, several factors worked in the company's favor: the agent had not been made known to first-level supervision; he reported to his own agency and filed his reports in writing; the identity of the substance was confirmed by the local police; and the evidence at the hearing was comprehensive.

The arbitrator was not impressed by the testimony of the individual grievants, characterizing it as inconsistent and contradictory. He found no reason to mitigate the discharge. The grievances were denied.

A COMPANY RUNS
ITS OWN DRUG BUST

Sometimes, management will attempt to run its own covert operation. U.S. Borax hired undercover investigators for just such a purpose. The two investigators were told to ferret out and expose as many drug users as possible. They identified seventeen employees as drug users or suppliers. This grievance involved one of them.

An investigator named Garcia reported that, on the morning of February 9, 1982, a worker sold him a quarter of an ounce of marijuana at a price of $40. The marijuana that he claimed to have received was neither identified nor preserved as evidence. Garcia said that he had used the marijuana as a prop in maintaining his cover as a drug user, but only after he had shown it to his company contact, who identified the contents of the bag as marijuana.

The grievant denied selling marijuana to Garcia or accepting any money from him. He said that he had been warned that Garcia was a "narc." When Garcia asked him where he could find "pot," the grievant told him that he did not know. He said that Garcia's accusation stemmed from tensions that had developed between them when they were working together.

No criminal charges were ever brought against this

worker, although some of the other employees had been charged. This grievant consistently said that he had been "set up" by Garcia.

The key issue was credibility. To sustain the discharge, the company had to show that the grievant had brought marijuana into the plant area to sell to Garcia. Under the company's rules, immediate discharge would result from "possession or use of intoxicating beverages or narcotics in the plant area."

The arbitrator, Frederic N. Richman, an attorney from Beverly Hills, California, pointed out that, in drug cases, the standard is one of clear and convincing evidence. "No lesser standard adequately serves when the effect of the discharge impacts the grievant's employability in the future."

Since the only evidence connecting the employee with the sale of marijuana was the testimony of Garcia, that standard had not been met. There had been ample opportunity to preserve the marijuana that Garcia claimed to have received from the grievant. Further, the identification of the substance as marijuana could not be given much weight because it was never tested. In any case, there was no proof, other than Garcia's testimony, that the drug was purchased from the grievant. The arbitrator concluded that the company had failed to meet its burden of proof. The grievant's record showed him to be a conscientious and hard-working employee. He was ordered reinstated with full back pay.

Most personnel departments are inexperienced in the sophisticated game of running covert drug investigations. U.S. Borax could have used professional help. On the other hand, when the police are brought in, a company should be prepared to surrender much of the control over the operation. This, too, can have unfortunate side effects, as the following case demonstrates.

A DRUG BUST CALLED MEG

During a countywide investigation into drug trafficking, the Metropolitan Enforcement Group (MEG), a joint task force of three local Ohio police departments, suspected that the Walker Manufacturing plant might be serving as a distribution center for a drug ring. The company agreed to allow one of MEG's undercover agents to investigate.

During April of 1982, when the investigator was brought into the plant, the personnel manager was pledged to secrecy. No one else in the plant knew about the agent. Beginning in July, the investigator reported purchases of marijuana but refused to identify the employees. The personnel manager asked for their names but was given no information. Finally, in early August, the company demanded that the investigation be concluded. The investigator left on August 12.

The task force then agreed to disclose the names of employees who had sold or smoked marijuana in the plant. Nineteen employees were identified by the agent. This information was given in confidence to the personnel director. He was asked to take no action because it might jeopardize the continuing MEG investigation. He agreed.

At this company, possession or consumption of "controlled substances" was prohibited and was subject to discipline. Controlled substances, under the Ohio criminal code, included marijuana. On November 3, the company posted a reminder notice about its drug policy, stating that violators would be severely disciplined.

On December 11, MEG conducted a large-scale drug sweep. The persons suspected of being drug dealers were arrested. On the following Monday, the company's personnel director began to interview the nineteen workers who had been identified earlier by the investigator. The union president was present.

Walker Manufacturing decided to discharge the employees who had sold drugs in the plant or had used drugs on company premises on five or more occasions. Six employees, including the grievant, were discharged for these violations. The other thirteen got twenty-five-day suspensions.

The grievant's use of marijuana on nine separate occasions was not in dispute, but the union argued that suspension was appropriate for him as well. The work rule stated that an employee committing an infraction "shall be subject to discharge, suspension or written or oral reprimand as appropriate."

The arbitrator, Professor Alan Miles Ruben of Cleveland–Marshall College of Law, Cleveland State University, disagreed with the union, concluding that discharge was appropriate. The employee had been with the company less than two months. There was no basis for concluding that he was innocent or had been induced to smoke by the investigator.

The union also contended that the discharge was discriminatory since only six of the nineteen employees who violated the work rules were discharged. Picking five or more occasions as the criterion for habitual use seemed arbitrary. There was no showing that five incidents constituted "habitual" use. In addition, it was mere chance that the investigator happened to be assigned to this worker's shift.

The arbitrator admitted that the number five carried no special magic. Nevertheless, the company "should not be criticized for giving some employees a second chance based upon objective criteria of lesser frequency of use of the controlled substance." With regard to the grievant's bad luck in being on the same shift as the agent, the arbitrator said that there was no indication that the company had targeted a specific group of workers.

The union argued that the company delayed almost four months before imposing sanctions and, by doing so, waived its right to complain. The arbitrator found that the delay was reasonable since it was not within the company's control. MEG would not identify the offenders initially, and later did so only in return for a promise that the company would restrain itself. As soon as the police raids were carried out, the company took action. In any case, the grievant was not prejudiced by the delay.

Ruben supported the company, explaining that marijuana is a mood-altering drug. It impairs judgment and motor coordination. Its use by employees who operate machinery creates a safety hazard. Research findings suggest that employees under its influence operate at less than their normal ability and are more likely to be injured. He added that trafficking in marijuana was a criminal offense in Ohio, engaged in by organized crime. The use of the drug by employees holds the risk of introducing such a link to the work environment.

"For these reasons, arbitrators have held over the years that the smoking of marijuana in the plant constitutes a disciplinary offense, even in the absence of a specific prohibition in the plant rules . . . . Several decisions have upheld management's right to impose a summary discharge without attempting corrective discipline." Here, the work rules themselves stated that use of a controlled substance could be grounds for discharge. The arbitrator denied the grievance.

SUMMARY

Undercover drug investigations are risky. Cases reporting them often read like thrillers on late-night television. What is important to remember is that, whether an employer initiates an operation or is dragooned into one by a local narcotics squad, covert investigations can destroy plant morale. Do not use them unless you are willing to pay that price.

As these cases indicate, the arbitrator will want to be sure that there is a plant rule against the possession, sale, or use of drugs, and that the employer has enforced it. Then, proof of the violation must be demonstrated by clear and convincing evidence, with the testimony of the covert agent corroborated by other sources whenever possible.

CITATIONS

Is It Smart to Send in the Narcs?: Lockheed Corporation *and* Aeronautical Industrial District Lodge 727, 75 *Labor Arbitration Reports* (LA) 1081 (1981).

Caveat Vendor: Certified Grocers of Illinois, Inc. *and* International Brotherhood of Teamsters, Chauffeurs, Warehousemen and Helpers of America, Local 738, 281 *Summary of Labor Arbitration Awards* (AAA) 9 (1982).

Fired for Flogging Two Black Mollies on Campus: State University of New York, University College at Buffalo, New York *and* Civil Service Employees Association, Inc., 74 LA 299 (1980).

A Videotaped Pot Party in the Locker Room: Mt. Sinai Medical Center *and* American Federation of State, County and Municipal Employees, Ohio Council 8, Local 2679, *Labor Arbitration in Government* (LAIG) 3731 (1986).

If You Must Do It, Do It Right!: Abex Corporation *and* United Automobile, Aerospace and Agricultural Implement Workers of America, Local 1991, 291 AAA 4 (1983).

A Company Runs Its Own Drug Bust: United States Borax & Chemical Corporation *and* International Longshoremen's and Warehousemen's Union, Mine, Mineral and Processing Workers, Local 30, 84 LA 32 (1985).

A Drug Bust Called MEG: Walker Manufacturing Company *and* United Automobile, Aerospace and Agricultural Implement Workers of America, Local 1927, 312 AAA 1 (1985).

CHAPTER 7

Possession and Use

The cases in this chapter involve employees who were disciplined for bringing drugs into the workplace or for being caught using drugs. These cases were not identified as part of a covert investigation, but came to the attention of the employer during the normal course of the working day. How did the employers deal with these problems? Here, the arbitrators had to decide whether the employer took the proper action and if the discipline meted out was fair and in accordance with the applicable rules. The arbitrators also had to determine whether, in the subsequent arbitration, the employer met its burden of proving the case.

Once again, the reader has an opportunity to second-guess management's decision. Ask yourself whether the employer handled these incidents properly. If mistakes were made, how did they affect the arbitrator's decision?

FIRED FOR FLUSHING THE TOILET

Michigan Consolidated Gas Company received a call from a customer on April 28, 1982, claiming that a uniformed serviceman was exchanging white packets for money. The complaint specified that the serviceman had been seen on April 26, 27, and 28, peddling white packets to children in the neighborhood. The customer was angry, threatening to call the media. She described the serviceman and gave the number of the truck. Company records disclosed that the truck had been signed out to a particular serviceman but was not in its assigned work area. The call was referred to a company investigator.

Four management officials then intercepted the serviceman at a stop to which the dispatcher directed him. One of the managers commandeered the truck, which was inspected and found not to contain white packets, although there was an unopened pint of vodka. The serviceman was escorted back to the main station for interrogation.

A shop steward was called into the meeting. The serviceman was informed of the charges. He refused to submit to a search of his clothing or to empty his pockets. The company, however, demanded that the employee return his uniform so that the investigator could look for drugs. He was told to go to the locker room to disrobe. When he did so, he was followed by an entourage.

On entering the room, the employee headed directly for a toilet stall. The investigator stopped him. The serviceman explained that he had to urinate. The investigator suggested that he use a urinal. The serviceman said that he did not want an audience. The investigator was concerned that he might dispose of evidence. He told the man not to flush the toilet. After the door to the stall closed, the general supervisor gave the man a direct order "not to flush the toilet."

As the group watched under the door, the grievant took off his shoes. They heard water running, and then the toilet flushed. Their directions had been to no avail. In response to questions, the serviceman stated that he was brought up to be clean. He then emptied his pockets and returned his uniform to the investigator. Nothing incriminating was found in the search.

Afterward, the complaining witness who triggered the investigation failed to come forward. Fear of reprisal was her excuse. Thus, the company had no proof of the alleged sale. The company lacked any evidence of drug dealing. The remainder of its case was based on its claim that the serviceman had disobeyed a direct order not to flush the toilet. When the man was terminated, the union filed a grievance.

Arbitrator M. David Keefe of Michigan, a commissioner of the Federal Mediation and Conciliation Service in the mid-fifties, described management's handling of this affair as Keystone Kops bungling through a Mack Sennett movie. The investigator proved that he did not understand labor relations when he requested that the grievant voluntarily submit to a search, empty his pockets, use the urinal instead of the toilet stall, and refrain from flushing the toilet. When a search is to be made, management should give an order requiring compliance. It would be sufficient to tell the worker to empty his pockets or face suspension on a charge of insubordination. By failing to take a firm stance with this employee, the investigator created a "sanctuary of permissiveness." It was not until the general supervisor gave a direct order not to flush the toilet that the grievant was obliged to show his hand. When the toilet flushed, according to Keefe, it was the grievant's credibility, not the company's, that went down the drain. The grievant disobeyed a direct order. Keefe felt that his explanation was "insipid and flippant under the existing circumstances." The grievance was denied.

Management should insist that an employee disclose whatever is reasonably required to show violation of the working rules. An employer has the right to enforce its policies and to order employees to cooperate in that effort.

QUAALUDE ABUSE IN PARADISE

The grievant in this case was a delivery-truck driver on the Waikiki route in Hawaii. On May 22, 1981, he brought his truck to the loading dock early in the morning and then went upstairs to the washroom. He remained there for an unusually long time, and his truck was ready to go. A supervisor was sent to check on him. The driver was in a stall with the door closed. When asked if he was all right, he said that he felt a bit ill.

A few minutes later, the supervisor saw the driver come out of the commode; there was blood on his wrists and all over the toilet area. An ambulance was called. During the twenty minutes it took to arrive, supervisors tried to stop the bleeding. The grievant was taken to Queens Hospital, where it was later determined that he had done extensive damage to his right wrist in an apparent suicide attempt. The grievant admitted having taken several Quaalude pills. He told the anesthesiologist that he had been drinking as well. He was released from the hospital on May 27.

The company waited until the employee was out of the hospital. Management then conferred about the proper action. It considered four factors: the self-injury; the damage to the right wrist reported by the doctor, which would require a long recovery; the impact on other employees, customers, and on the company itself; and the grievant's past record, notable for poor attendance and a recognized drug problem. After discussions with the union, the company obtained a medical opinion that it was doubtful whether the grievant would be able to return to his job. The grievant was discharged on June 2.

The issue before the arbitrator, Professor Thomas Q. Gilson of the University of Hawaii College of Business Administration, was whether the employer had just cause for discharge after discovering that the grievant had been using drugs to the point of near suicide. At the hearing, the grievant admitted that he had a serious drug addiction and that he often consumed up to twenty Quaaludes a day. Quaaludes then cost five dollars each—a $100-a-day habit.

The union contended that the grievant's suicide attempt was caused by a mental illness fostered by excessive drug use, which the grievant had now overcome. The company, however, was concerned about the effect of the suicide attempt on other drivers, as well as the company's reputation with its customers. The grievant had violated two work rules that morning that were punishable by discharge. The first rule prohibited employees from deliberately provoking injuries to themselves on company premises during working hours; the second violation was being under the influence of alcoholic beverages, narcotics, or barbiturates on company premises during working hours. The grievant's prior record included complaints about his behavior when he was thought to be under the influence of drugs or alcohol.

The arbitrator was convinced that the grievant did

violate both of the rules cited by the company. Taking drugs to the point of mental imbalance and attempted suicide is no excuse for violating such rules. Neither the grievant's mental illness nor any speculations about his psychological recovery justified setting aside the penalty imposed. In any case, medical testimony showed that it would be a long time before the grievant could drive a truck. Therefore, this grievance was denied.

BURNED AND THEN BURNED AGAIN

A relatively new employee was working on the night shift on April 1, 1979. While doing so, he was splashed with sodium, a caustic substance that singed his clothing and inflicted second-degree burns on his body. It was not his fault—simply a risk of the operation. The foreman helped him out of his clothing, and the worker was taken to a shower. Afterward, the worker asked for his locker key so he could get his street clothes. As the foreman removed the keys and other items from the still-smoldering clothing, he discovered a half-empty package of cigarettes, a few pieces of candy, two meal tickets, and a "home-made" cigarette that later proved to be marijuana. The worker denied that the cigarette was his.

Because of his burns, the worker was away from work for a week. On April 9, he was notified that he had been discharged pursuant to a company rule that stated, "Carrying intoxicants, drugs or hallucinogenic agents or being under the influence of such items while in the plant can be cause for immediate dismissal."

The union challenged the company rule on two grounds. The rule was unknown to the employee. He had never seen the booklet "The Safe Worker at Ethyl," in which the rule appears. Nor did he recall hearing about the rule at an orientation session. Anyway, according to the union, the rule was unreasonable. In Texas, the possession of less than two ounces of marijuana is not a felony, only a misdemeanor subject to a fine.

The union contended that in the industrial world, marijuana is considered no worse than alcohol. In any case, the rule had never been consistently enforced. Drug and alcohol cases should be treated the same. Testimony at the hearing showed that employees who came to work drunk were merely told to go home. No discipline was imposed. The union argued that the same action should have been applied here.

The arbitrator, William S. Hart of Dayton, Ohio, a former Air Force labor specialist who subsequently moved to Seattle and later to Japan, said that whether or not the grievant had received a copy of the rule, he should have known that his conduct could result in discipline.

> The wrong in question is such a general prohibition in business and society that it can be assumed that employees are aware of it. There are certain acts that every mature person must know are prohibited in the workplace. These need not be incorporated in plant rules to be the basis of discipline.

The second question involved the reasonableness of the rule and the consistency with which it was applied. Hart cited Frank Elkouri and Edna Asper Elkouri's *How Arbitration Works*: "The test of reasonableness of a plant rule is whether or not the rule is reasonably related to the legitimate objective of management." Here, management was concerned about protecting its workers from accidents that might

occur from the use of drugs. Prohibiting drug possession follows logically from prohibiting its use. The arbitrator ruled that it was reasonable for the company
to have a rule against possession of marijuana.

Inconsistent application of drug rules may prompt
an arbitrator to overturn discipline, however. The
union proved disparate treatment. The company admitted that in the past some workers had appeared for
work under the influence of alcohol and been sent
home. The arbitrator pointed out that the company rule
did not distinguish between alcohol and drugs and,
therefore, both kinds of violations should be given the
same treatment. Employee job performance can be impaired by either alcohol or marijuana. Treating alcohol
use with tolerance but discharging the employee for
marijuana possession was improper, according to the
arbitrator.

Since possession of marijuana was a violation of
the company rule, however, the grievant received no
back pay for time lost. Discharge would be appropriate
if he brought marijuana into the plant a second time.

Was the arbitrator influenced by the fact that this
grievant had been injured in an industrial accident?
Would the result have been different if he had been
caught with the marijuana as he entered the plant?
Was the arbitrator looking for some way to take this
employee off the hook?

TWO SACKERS SACKED FOR POT

One of the issues in the previous case was whether
the use of marijuana should be treated on a par with
alcohol in terms of disciplinary action. The answer may

depend on the company rule, as above, or on how the arbitrator views the potential hazards associated with marijuana and alcohol. Some arbitrators believe that marijuana is no more dangerous than alcohol. A minority even treat marijuana as less threatening than alcohol. Alcoholism is frequently described in arbitrators' opinions as an "illness" or "disease," whereas marijuana use may be described as "recreational." On the other hand, arbitrators sometimes note that marijuana is a drug whose sale or use is punishable by law. Moderate use of alcohol is legal, at least for adults in most jurisdictions.

The grievants in this case were employed as "sackers" at a Kroger retail store in Montgomery County, Ohio. Their responsibilities included carrying groceries to automobiles parked in the store's lot and collecting shopping carts left there. They also had to clean up spills and sort empty-bottle returns. They wore smocks with name tags and the Kroger logo.

On February 26, 1981, two employees were spotted by a supervisor, sitting in a truck parked in the company lot. One was smoking what appeared to be a cigarette, which he held between his thumb and index finger. He handed the cigarette to the other sacker, who also inhaled. The supervisor approached them, smelled marijuana, and asked them if they were on a "joint break." They answered yes. He reported the incident to the store manager, who told him to bring the sackers to his office. After a brief meeting, both admitted that they were using marijuana and were dismissed. The manager asked them if they wanted him to call the police. "No," they said. Nor did they want their parents involved. When they left the store, they thanked the manager for not calling the police. A few days later, however, first one and then the other asked for his job back. The company refused. Grievances were filed and, when not resolved, submitted to arbitration.

The question before the arbitrator was whether dismissal was too severe for the offense. The Kroger rule at the time of the grievants' discharge prohibited "possession or use of illegal drugs in the workplace as well as being under the influence of such drugs." The rule did not define illegal drugs, but the arbitrator, Rankin M. Gibson, a lawyer and former judge from Columbus, Ohio, said that marijuana was such a drug, citing the state criminal code.

The store gave three reasons for discharging the grievants: customers would be offended; safety considerations; and the illegality of the conduct. The union, on the other hand, pointed out that marijuana smoking was widespread and generally decriminalized. The company had not terminated workers who were caught drinking on duty, and lately had taken a more flexible approach toward the use or possession of marijuana. The language that called for dismissal as the penalty had been eliminated.

The arbitrator agreed with the union. "The change in the rule places the penalty for violating the drug portion on the same level as the rule concerning the use of alcohol." Consequently, the arbitrator found that the company did not have just cause to dismiss the grievants for their first offense. In formulating the change in its rules, Kroger must have contemplated that drug use would be treated much the same as drinking.

Both employees had good work records during their three or four years with the company. They testified that they each had taken one puff on the joint. There was no proof that their job performance had been adversely affected. Nor was there any proof that a customer had seen them or had been offended by the incident. The grievances were upheld.

A TRACTOR–TRAILER DRIVER GETS ANOTHER CHANCE

Signal Delivery provides trucking services for Sears Roebuck. The grievant in this case had driven for the company for some twenty-two years prior to his discharge on May 3, 1985. On that day, while driving his tractor–trailer, he had two accidents, one in the morning and another in the afternoon. His supervisor gave him two accident-report forms that evening as he clocked out. When the driver returned with the completed forms, the supervisor smelled alcohol on his breath. At first, the employee denied that he had been drinking, explaining that the smell was from a cough drop. The supervisor told him that he could smell both the cough drop and the liquor. He again asked the driver whether he had been drinking. The driver then admitted having had one beer at lunch. He asked the supervisor to let the incident pass, but the supervisor said that he could not because of the possible connection between the accidents and his drinking. He suggested that the driver submit to a blood test. The driver agreed to do so.

They drove to one hospital that was too busy to give the test. They then drove to another. After waiting ten minutes, the driver was taken to an outpatient room for the test. After several minutes, he came out again, saying that he had decided not to take it. They returned to the terminal. That night, the supervisor prepared a report of the events. Based on that report, the driver was terminated on May 6 for insubordination and being intoxicated on the job.

In its presentation in arbitration, the company cited a government safety regulation: No person shall "consume an intoxicating liquor, regardless of its

alcoholic content, or be under the influence of an intoxicating liquor within four hours before going on duty
or operating . . . a motor vehicle." The company required its employees to adhere to such regulations.

The union contended that the grievant was not told
that he would be discharged for not taking the blood
test. He never received a direct order to take the test.
In any case, there was no evidence that he was intoxicated. Drinking one beer should not be a basis for terminating a long-service employee.

The arbitrator, Edward M. Wies, a long-time
mediator with the Federal Mediation and Conciliation
Service, was not convinced that the grievant had been
intoxicated. No evidence was submitted to show that
he was impaired, except for the smell of alcohol on his
breath. "On the day in question, the grievant admitted
drinking a beer during his lunch hour. The evidence
is clear that he then went on for the next four hours
to satisfactorily perform his job" (satisfactory except
for a second accident with his tractor–trailer). He
pointed out that the company had published no rules
on the use of alcohol. On the other hand, the grievant
should have known not to drink before driving. Nevertheless, Wies concluded that termination was too
drastic a penalty. Even though the driver was guilty
of a serious infraction, he reinstated him without back
pay. The lost time could be viewed as a suspension for
drinking on the job.

Here, the company had relied on federal regulations rather than its own work rules—another example of how statutory law can become involved in arbitration cases. For years, arbitrators have argued
about whether they are authorized to consider such
laws in reaching their decisions. In drug cases, this will
continue to be a problem. For example, does an
employer have the legal right to test an employee for

drugs or alcohol? California has a privacy provision in its constitution. A statute in that state forbids medical providers from releasing the results of tests for alcohol or drugs without the consent of the employee. California residents cannot be discriminated against in their employment for refusing to give such a release. This may create serious impediments for an employer who wants to investigate an accident thought to have been caused by drug abuse. What if an employee refuses to sign an authorization for the release of drug-test results to an employer? Can the employer terminate such an employee for insubordination?

CITATIONS

Fired for Flushing the Toilet: Michigan Consolidated Gas Company *and* Gas Workers Service Employees International Union, Local 80, 80 *Labor Arbitration Reports* (LA) 693 (1984).

Quaalude Abuse in Paradise: Meadow Gold Dairies of Hawaii *and* Hawaii Teamsters and Allied Workers, Local 996, 283 *Summary of Labor Arbitration Awards* (AAA) 10 (1982).

Burned and Then Burned Again: Ethyl Corporation *and* Oil, Chemical and Atomic Workers International Union, Local 4-16000, 74 LA 953 (1980).

Two Sackers Sacked for Pot: Kroger Company *and* United Food and Commercial Workers International Union, Local 1552, 9 *Labor Arbitration Information System* (LAIS) 1069 (1982).

A Tractor–Trailer Driver Gets Another Chance: Signal Delivery Service *and* Chicago Truck Drivers, Helpers and Warehouse Workers Union, Independent, 86 LA 75 (1986).

Conclusion

The cases in this book describe incident after incident where employees and managers have become embroiled in the human problems of drugs and alcohol. Some of the disciplined workers have a deeply embedded addiction and are unable to rid themselves of a habit that has made it impossible to carry out their duties. Others, almost by chance, are caught while engaging in casual use.

The cast of characters is varied: alcoholics caught in the net of their addiction or illness; recreational users of marijuana with small amounts of that substance discovered in their cars, their lunch boxes, or their work clothes; dealers who supplement their salaries by supplying coworkers with drugs. None of the grievants in this book can be called "kingpins" in the drug industry. They are merely people who have been caught up in a relationship with alcohol and drugs that places them in a confrontation with their employer.

For some of these grievants, the union is able to provide an effective defense, putting the employer to the test. In a non-union setting, they would have no champion. Under a collective bargaining agreement, they have the right to submit their case to an impartial arbitrator, a person experienced in industrial relations, sympathetic both to the individual rights of workers and to the managerial needs of employers. In these cases, the reader can appraise the thought processes of the many labor arbitrators who have been mutually selected by labor and management to decide these difficult cases.

Do these cases indicate that drugs and alcohol are a major concern of American industry? Perhaps, but they must be considered in their context. No matter how many millions of Americans drink liquor or smoke pot, the working day is generally substance free. Most employees show up ready to work; reporting for duty under the influence is relatively rare.

At the same time, many Americans concede that drugs and alcohol create serious problems. They express concern about drugs being used and sold in their communities and even in their places of work. They know alcoholics and the mess they make of their lives —drunken drivers, broken families, health problems. They worry about the evils of criminal drug rings. They know many people who use marijuana and other drugs and would like to see the drug problem solved.

A substantial number of people support drug testing for new employees, airline pilots, police officers, surgeons, and truck drivers, and possibly for role models such as public officials, teachers, and professional athletes. Many might also support random testing for all employees and students.

What does this portend for the future? Are we headed toward a time when technological improvements in drug testing will make it possible to scan people electronically for drugs and alcohol, without requiring a urine specimen or a blood sample—allowing indiscriminate checks, not just for drugs, but for infectious diseases and other medical information? Only time will tell.

At any rate, we are not there yet. Providing a urine sample is unpleasant for both the person being tested and for the supervisor who must monitor the sampling. Blood samples are equally unpleasant. Testing for drugs and alcohol is intrusive, distorting the relationship between worker and employer. Even more so, the placement of covert investigators in the working environment weakens the atmosphere of trust that forms the basis of healthy employee morale.

As we have seen in case after case, employers adopt harsh and punitive policies when dealing with drug abuse, while often condoning seemingly equivalent abuse of alcohol. Why this diversity? Will arbitrators continue to dance to the melody of this cultural quandary? In some of the cases described in this book, arbitrators have refused to treat marijuana differently than alcohol. Will that be the pattern for the future?

The cases in this book do not reflect normal working life. Arbitration cases are the autopsies of industrial strife, the battle zone between work rules that prohibit drug use or possession and the relatively few workers who get caught violating such rules. Alcoholism is all-too common, but many heavy drinkers are able to maintain their employment. The use of drugs is also prevalent, but most users control their habits. For those who do not, one can picture labor relations as a sieve, with chronic alcoholics, drug addicts, pushers, and other violators dropping out at the bottom.

In these cases, the reader has seen the process at work. Did the union adequately protect the rights of its members? Could it have made a better case? Did the employer justify its actions? Was the arbitrator correct in evaluating the evidence, in analyzing the case, in reaching the right decision? You be the judge!

Bibliography

Alcohol & Drugs in the Workplace: Costs, Controls, and Controversies. A BNA Special Report. Rockville, MD: Bureau of National Affairs, 1986.

"Alcoholism in Industry—Discussion." In *Arbitration—1975: Proceedings of the Twenty-Eighth Annual Meeting, National Academy of Arbitrators . . . April 28–May 3, 1975,* pp. 125–137. Washington, DC: Bureau of National Affairs, 1976.

Andrewson, Dale E. "Arbitral Views of Alcoholism Cases." *Personnel Journal,* vol. 58, no. 5 (May 1979), pp. 318–322.

Bell, Cathleen G. "Drug Testing Issues in Arbitration." *Detroit College of Law Review,* vol. 1989, issue 3 (Fall 1989), pp. 899–930.

Bornstein, Tim. "Drug and Alcohol Issues in the Workplace: An Arbitrator's Perspective." *The Arbitration Journal,* vol. 39, no. 3 (September 1984), pp. 19–24.

_____. "Second Look at Substance Abuse in Arbitration." *Proceedings of New York University Annual National Conference on Labor,* pp. 10:1–10:17. New York: Little, Brown, 1989.

Casey, Dennis L. "Drug Testing in a Unionized Environment." *Employee Relations Law Journal,* vol 13, no. 4 (Spring 1988), pp. 599–613.

Clark, Leroy D. "Substance Abuse: The Problem That Won't Go Away. Part III. Drug Abuse in the Workplace: Arbitration in the Context of a National Solution of Decriminalization." In *Arbitration 1987: The Academy at 40—Proceedings of the Fortieth Annual Meeting, National Academy of Arbitrators . . . May 25–29, 1987*, pp. 93–106. Washington, DC: Bureau of National Affairs, 1988.

Cone, Lorynn A. "Public Policies against Drug Use." *Labor Law Journal*, vol. 40, issue 4 (April 1989), pp. 243–247.

Denenberg, Tia Schneider. "The Arbitration of Alcohol and Drug Abuse Cases." *The Arbitration Journal*, vol. 35, no. 4 (December 1980), pp. 16–21.

_____. "The Arbitration of Employee Drug Abuse Cases: An Arbitrator's Perspective." In *Arbitration—Promise and Performance: Proceedings of the Thirty-Sixth Annual Meeting, National Academy of Arbitrators . . . May 24–27, 1983*, pp. 90–100. Washington, DC: Bureau of National Affairs, 1984.

_____. "Arbitration of Employee Substance Abuse Rehabilitation Issues." *Arbitration Journal*, vol. 46, no. 1 (March 1991), pp. 17–33.

_____. "Drug and Alcohol Abuse." In *Proceedings of New York University Thirty-Seventh Annual Conference on Labor . . . June 6, 7 and 8, 1984*, pp. 14-1–14-19. New York: Matthew Bender, 1984.

_____. "Drug Testing from the Arbitrator's Perspective." *Nova Law Review*, vol. 11, no. 2 (Winter 1987), pp. 371–413.

_____ and R. V. Denenberg. *Alcohol and Drugs: Issues in the Workplace*. Washington, DC: Bureau of National Affairs, 1983.

_____. "Employee Drug Testing and the Arbitrator: What Are the Issues?" *The Arbitration Journal*, vol. 42, no. 2 (June 1987), pp. 19–31.

Denis, Martin K. "Privacy Rights and Drug Testing: Is There a Conflict?" *Employment Relations Today*, vol. 13, no. 4 (Winter 1986/1987), pp. 347–358.

"Drug Abuse." In *Grievance Guide*, 6th ed., pp. 90–94. Washington, DC: Bureau of National Affairs, 1982.

Dugan, Robert D. "Affirmative Action for Alcoholics and Addicts?" *Employee Relations Law Journal*, vol. 5, no. 2 (Autumn 1979), pp. 235–244.

"Employee Drug Testing Policies in Police Departments." Rockville, MD: National Institute of Justice, 198?.

Florman, Phyllis E. "Testing for Drugs and AIDS in the Workplace." *Fourth Annual Labor and Employment Law Institute, School of Law, University of Louisville . . .* Apr. 29–30, 1987, pp. 36–45. Littleton, CO: Rothman, 1988.

Godwin, Donald F. "The Problems of Alcoholism in Industry." In *Arbitration—1975: Proceedings of the Twenty-Eighth Annual Meeting, National Academy of Arbitrators . . . April 28–May 3, 1975*, pp. 97–103. Washington, DC: Bureau of National Affairs, 1976.

Goldsmith, Willis J. "Substance Abuse: The Problem That Won't Go Away. Part II. A Management Perspective." In *Arbitration 1987: The Academy at 40—Proceedings of the Fortieth Annual Meeting, National Academy of Arbitrators . . . May 25–29, 1987*, pp. 84–93. Washington, DC: Bureau of National Affairs, 1988.

Greenbaum, Marcia L. "The 'Disciplinatrator,' The 'Arbichiatrist,' and the 'Social Psychotrator': An Inquiry into How Arbitrators Deal with a Grievant's Personal Problems and the Extent to Which They Affect the Award." *The Arbitration Journal*, vol. 37, no. 4 (December 1982), pp. 51–64.

Hartstein, Barry A. "Drug Testing in the Workplace: A Primer for Employees." *Employee Relations Law Journal*, vol. 12, no. 4 (Spring 1987), pp. 577–608.

Hill, Barbara J. "Alcoholism and the World of Work." In *Arbitration—1975: Proceedings of the Twenty-Eighth Annual Meeting, National Academy of Arbitrators . . . April 28–May 3, 1975*, pp. 93–97. Washington, DC: Bureau of National Affairs, 1976.

Hill, Charlotte M. "Arbitrator's Response to Dismissal of Alcoholic Employees." *Detroit College of Law Review*, vol. 1989, issue 3 (Fall 1989), pp. 1213–1233.

Hoffman, Joan W. and Ken Jennings. "Will Drug Testing in Sports Play for Industry?" *Personnel Journal*, vol. 66, no. 5 (May 1987), pp. 52–59.

Hopson, Edwin S. "Alcohol and Drug Abuse Cases in Arbitration." In William F. Dolson, ed., *Second Annual Labor and Employment Law Institute*, 1986, pp. 275–290. Littleton, CO: Fred B. Rothman & Co., 1986.

Hoyt, David W., Robert E. Finnigan, Thomas Nee, Theodore F. Shults and Thorne J. Butler. "Drug Testing in the Workplace—Are Methods Legally Defensible? A Survey of Experts, Arbitrators, and Testing Laboratories." *Journal of the American Medical Association*, vol. 258, no. 4 (July 1987), pp. 504–509.

"Intoxication & Alcoholism." In *Grievance Guide*, 6th ed., pp. 84–89. Washington, DC: Bureau of National Affairs, 1982.

Kahn, Steven C. "Drugs and Alcohol in the Work Place." *Employment Relations Today*, vol. 12, no. 2 (Summer 1985), pp. 127–136.

Landis, Brook I. "Discharging the Drug Dealer . . . and Making It Stick." *Security Management*, vol. 3, no. 8 (August 1986), pp. 68–70.

Lawson, Eric, Jr. "Discipline of Substance Abusers: An Arbitral Response." *New York State Bar Journal*, vol. 59, no. 7 (November 1987), pp. 36–40, 59.

Loomis, Lloyd. "Employee Assistance Programs: Their Impact on Arbitration and Litigation of Termination Cases." *Employee Relations Law Journal*, vol. 12, no. 2 (Autumn 1986), pp. 275–288.

————. "Drug Testing." *Workplace Guide to Designing Practical Policies and Winning Arbitrations*. Washington, DC: Bureau of National Affairs, 1990.

McDermott, Thomas J. "Drugs, Bombs and Bomb Scares, and Personnel Attire." In *Labor Arbitration at the Quarter-Century Mark, Proceedings of the Twenty-Fifth Annual Meeting. National Academy of Arbitrators . . . April 4–7, 1972,* pp. 252-272. Washington, DC: Bureau of National Affairs, 1973.

McHugh, William A., Jr. "Substance Abuse: The Problem That Won't Go Away. Part I. A Labor Perspective." In *Arbitration 1987: The Academy at 40—Proceedings of the Fortieth Annual Meeting, National Academy of Arbitrators . . . May 25–29, 1987,* pp. 67–83. Washington, DC: Bureau of National Affairs, 1988.

Marmo, Michael. "Alcoholism, Drug Addiction, and Mental Illness: The Use of Rehabilitative Remedies in Arbitration." *Labor Law Journal,* vol. 32, no. 8 (August 1981), pp. 491–497.

_____. "Arbitrators Consider Employee Drug Abuse: An Illness?" *Mid-Atlantic Journal of Business,* vol. 23, no. 1 (Winter 1984/85), pp. 21–33.

_____. "Arbitrators View Alcoholic Employees: Discipline or Rehabilitation?" *The Arbitration Journal,* vol. 37, no. 1 (March 1982), pp. 17–27.

_____. "Arbitrators View Problem Employees: Discipline or Rehabilitation?" *Journal of Contemporary Law,* vol. 9 (1983), pp. 41–79.

Masters, Marick F. "Drug-Testing in the Federal Sector: The Negotiability Controversy." *Labor Law Journal,* vol. 39, no. 5 (May 1988), pp. 312–319.

Masters, Richard L. and Kenneth B. Cooper. "The Arbitration of Employee Drug Abuse Cases: Some Special Issues Peculiar to Air Carrier Pilots." In *Arbitration—Promise and Performance: Proceedings of the Thirty-Sixth Annual Meeting, National Academy of Arbitrators . . . May 24–27, 1983,* pp. 101–120. Washington, DC: Bureau of National Affairs, 1984.

Mehlsack, Barbara. "Drug Testing as an Arbitral Issue." *Proceedings of New York University Annual National Conference on Labor*, pp. 4:1–4:20. New York: Little, Brown, 1987.

Miller, Thomas R. and Susan M. Oliver. "Just Cause and The Troubled Employee." *Proceedings of the Annual Meeting, National Academy of Arbitrators*, pp. 34–67. Washington, DC: Bureau of National Affairs, 1988.

Murphy, Betty Southard. "How to Protect Employees Who Are Tested for Drug and Alcohol Abuse." *The Practical Lawyer*, vol. 33, no. 3 (April 1987), pp. 27–40.

Redeker, James R. and Jonathan A. Segal. "How to Protect Employers Who Test for Drug and Alcohol Abuse." *The Practical Lawyer*, vol. 33, no. 3 (April 1987), pp. 13–26.

Roberts, Thomas T. "Sports Arbitration." *Industrial Relations Law Journal*, vol. 10, no. 1 (Winter 1988), pp. 8–11.

Schmedemann, Deborah A. "Unions and Urinalysis. (Drug Testing Symposium.)" *William Mitchell Law Review*, vol. 14, no. 2 (Spring 1988), pp. 277–336.

Simons, Jesse. "Alcoholism, Drug Abuse and Excessive Absences." In *Proceedings of New York University Thirty-Second Annual Conference on Labor . . . June 13, 14 and 15, 1979*, pp. 125–137. New York: Matthew Bender, 1980.

Somers, Gerald G. "Alcohol and the Just Cause for Discharge." In *Arbitration—1975: Proceedings of the Twenty-Eighth Annual Meeting, National Academy of Arbitrators . . . April 28–May 3, 1975*, pp. 103–117. Washington, DC: Bureau of National Affairs, 1976.

Spencer, Janet Maleson. "The Developing Notion of Employer Responsibility for the Alcoholic, Drug-Addicted or Mentally Ill Employee: An Examination under Federal and State Employment Statutes and Arbitration Decisions." *St. John's Law Review*, vol. 53, no. 4 (Summer 1979), pp. 659–720.

Thornicroft, Kenneth William. "Arbitrators, Social Values, and the Burden of Proof in Substance Abuse Discharge Cases." *Labor Law Journal*, vol. 40, issue 9 (September 1989), pp. 582–593.

Trice, Harrison M. "Alcoholism in Industry—Comment." In *Arbitration—1975: Proceedings of the Twenty-Eighth Annual Meeting, National Academy of Arbitrators . . . April 28–May 3, 1975*, pp. 120–125. Washington, DC: Bureau of National Affairs, 1976.

_____ and Paul M. Roman. *Spirits and Demons at Work: Alcohol and Other Drugs on the Job*. 2d ed. ILR Paperback no. 11. Ithaca: New York State School of Industrial and Labor Relations, Cornell University, 1979.

Tucker, Jerry R. "Alcoholism in Industry—Comment." In *Arbitration—1975: Proceedings of the Twenty-Eighth Annual Meeting, National Academy of Arbitrators . . . April 28–May 3, 1975*, pp. 117–119. Washington, DC: Bureau of National Affairs, 1976.

"Unrestricted Private Employee Drug Testing Programs: An Invasion of the Workers' Right to Privacy. Comments." *California Western Law Review*, vol. 23, no. 1 (Fall 1986), pp. 72–104.

Veglahn, Peter A. "What Is a Reasonable Drug Testing Program?: Insight from Arbitration Decisions." *Labor Law Journal*, vol. 39, no. 10 (October 1988), pp. 688–695.

Williamson, John D. "The Arbitration of Employee Drug Abuse Cases: An Industrial Relations Perspective." In *Arbitration—Promise and Performance: Proceedings of the Thirty-Sixth Annual Meeting, National Academy of Arbitrators . . . May 24–27, 1983*, pp. 120–127. Washington, DC: Bureau of National Affairs, 1984.

Wynns, Pat. "Arbitration Standards in Drug Discharge Cases." *The Arbitration Journal*, vol. 34, no. 2 (June 1979), pp. 19–27.

Voluntary Labor Arbitration Rules (Including Streamlined Labor Arbitration Rules)

As Amended and in Effect January 1, 1988

1. Agreement of Parties

The parties shall be deemed to have made these rules a part of their arbitration agreement whenever, in a collective bargaining agreement or submission, they have provided for arbitration by the American Arbitration Association (hereinafter the AAA) or under its rules. These rules and any amendment thereof shall apply in the form obtaining at the time the arbitration is initiated.

2. Name of Tribunal

Any tribunal constituted by the parties under these rules shall be called the Voluntary Labor Arbitration Tribunal.

3. Administrator

When parties agree to arbitrate under these rules and an arbitration is instituted thereunder, they thereby authorize the AAA to administer the arbitration. The authority and obligations of the administrator are as provided in the agreement of the parties and in these rules.

4. Delegation of Duties

The duties of the AAA may be carried out through such representatives or committees as the AAA may direct.

5. Panel of Labor Arbitrators

The AAA shall establish and maintain a Panel of Labor Arbitrators and shall appoint arbitrators therefrom, as hereinafter provided.

6. Office of Tribunal

The general office of the Voluntary Labor Arbitration Tribunal is the headquarters of the AAA, which may, however, assign the administration of an arbitration to any of its regional offices.

7. Initiation under an Arbitration Clause in a Collective Bargaining Agreement

Arbitration under an arbitration clause in a collective bargaining agreement under these rules may be initiated by either party in the following manner:

(a) By giving written notice to the other party of intention to arbitrate (Demand), which notice shall contain a statement setting forth the nature of the dispute and the remedy sought, and

(b) By filing at any regional office of the AAA three copies of said notice, together with a copy of the collective bargaining agreement, or such parts thereof as relate to the dispute, including the arbitration provisions. After the arbitrator is appointed, no new or different claim may be submitted except with the consent of the arbitrator and all other parties.

8. Answer

The party upon whom the Demand for arbitration is made may file an answering statement with the AAA within seven days after notice from the AAA, simultaneously sending a copy to the other party. If no answer is filed within the stated time, it will be assumed that the claim is denied. Failure to file an answer shall not operate to delay the arbitration.

9. Initiation under a Submission

Parties to any collective bargaining agreement may initiate an arbitration under these rules by filing at any regional office of the AAA two copies of a written agreement to arbitrate under these rules (Submission), signed by the parties and setting forth the nature of the dispute and the remedy sought.

10. Fixing of Locale

The parties may mutually agree upon the locale where the arbitration is to be held. If the locale is not designated in the collective bargaining agreement or Submission and, if there is a dispute as to the appropriate locale, the AAA shall have the power to determine the locale and its decision shall be binding.

11. Qualifications of Arbitrator

No person shall serve as a neutral arbitrator in any arbitration in which he or she has any financial personal interest in the result of the arbitration, unless the parties, in writing, waive such disqualification.

12. Appointment from Panel

If the parties have not appointed an arbitrator and have not provided any other method of appointment, the arbitrator shall be appointed in the following manner: Immediately after the filing of the Demand or Submission, the AAA shall submit simultaneously to each party an identical list of names of persons chosen from the Panel of Labor Arbitrators. Each party shall have seven days from the mailing date in which to cross off any names to which it objects, number the remaining names to indicate the order of preference, and return the list to the AAA. If a party does not return the list within the time specified, all persons named therein shall be deemed acceptable. From among the persons who have been approved on both lists, and in accordance with the designated order of mutual preference, the AAA shall invite the acceptance of an arbitrator to serve. If the parties fail to agree upon any of the persons named, if those named decline or are unable to act, or if for any other reason the appointment cannot be made from the submitted lists, the administrator shall have the power to make the appointment from among other members of the panel without the submission of any additional list.

13. Direct Appointment by Parties

If the agreement of the parties names an arbitrator or specifies a method of appointing an arbitrator, that designation or method shall be followed. The notice of appointment, with the name and address of such arbitrator, shall be filed with the AAA by the appointing party.

If the agreement specifies a period of time within which an arbitrator shall be appointed and any party fails to make such appointment within that period, the AAA may make the appointment.

If no period of time is specified in the agreement, the AAA shall notify the parties to make the appointment and if within seven days thereafter such arbitrator has not been so appointed, the AAA shall make the appointment.

14. Appointment of Neutral Arbitrator by Party-Appointed Arbitrators

If the parties have appointed their arbitrators, or if either or both of them have been appointed as provided in Section 13, and have authorized such arbitrators to appoint a neutral arbitrator within a specified time and no appointment is made within such time or any agreed extension thereof, the AAA may appoint a neutral arbitrator who shall act as chairperson.

If no period of time is specified for appointment of the neutral arbitrator and the parties do not make the appointment within seven days from the date of the appointment of the last party-appointed arbitrator, the AAA shall appoint such neutral arbitrator, who shall act as chairperson.

If the parties have agreed that the arbitrators shall appoint the neutral arbitrator from the panel, the AAA shall furnish to the party-appointed arbitrators, in the manner prescribed in Section 12, a list selected from the panel, and the appointment of the neutral arbitrator shall be made as prescribed in that section.

15. Number of Arbitrators

If the arbitration agreement does not specify the number of arbitrators, the dispute shall be heard and determined by one arbitrator, unless the parties otherwise agree.

16. Notice to Arbitrator of Appointment

Notice of the appointment of the neutral arbitrator shall be mailed to the arbitrator by the AAA and the signed acceptance of the arbitrator shall be filed with the AAA prior to the opening of the first hearing.

17. Disclosure by Arbitrator of Disqualification

Prior to accepting the appointment, the prospective neutral arbitrator shall disclose any circumstance likely to create a presumption of bias or that the arbitrator believes might disqualify him or her as an impartial arbitrator. Upon receipt of such information, the AAA shall immediately disclose it to the parties. If either party declines to waive the presumptive disqualification, the vacancy thus created shall be filled in accordance with the applicable provisions of these rules.

18. Vacancies

If any arbitrator should resign, die, withdraw, refuse, be unable, or be disqualified to perform the duties of office, the AAA shall, on proof satisfactory to it, declare the office vacant. Vacancies shall be filled in the same manner as that governing the making of the original appointment, and the matter shall be reheard by the new arbitrator.

19. Time and Place of Hearing

The arbitrator shall fix the time and place for each hearing. At least five days prior thereto, the AAA shall mail notice of the time and place of hearing to each party, unless the parties otherwise agree.

20. Representation by Counsel

Any party may be represented at the hearing by counsel or by another authorized representative.

21. Stenographic Record

Any party wishing a stenographic record shall make arrangements directly with a stenographer and shall notify the other parties of such arrangements in advance of the hearing. The requesting party or parties shall pay the cost of such record. If such transcript is agreed by the parties to be, or in appropriate cases determined by the arbitrator to be, the official record of the proceeding, it must be made available to the arbitrator and to the other party for inspection, at a time and place determined by the arbitrator.

22. Attendance at Hearings

Persons having a direct interest in the arbitration are entitled to attend hearings. The arbitrator shall have the power to require the retirement of any witness or witnesses during the testimony of other witnesses. It shall be discretionary with the arbitrator to determine the propriety of the attendance of any other person.

23. Adjournments

The arbitrator for good cause shown may adjourn the hearing upon the request of a party or upon his or her own initiative, and shall adjourn when all of the parties agree thereto.

24. Oaths

Before proceeding with the first hearing, each arbitrator may take an oath of office and, if required by law, shall do so. The arbitrator may require witnesses to testify under oath administered by any duly qualified person and, if required by law or requested by either party, shall do so.

25. Majority Decision

Whenever there is more than one arbitrator, all decisions of the arbitrators shall be by majority vote. The award shall also be made by majority vote unless the concurrence of all is expressly required.

26. Order of Proceedings

A hearing shall be opened by the filing of the oath of the arbitrator, where required; by the recording of the place, time, and date of the hearing and the presence of the arbitrator, the parties, and counsel, if any; and by the receipt by the arbitrator of the Demand and answer, if any, or the Submission.

Exhibits may, when offered by either party, be received in evidence by the arbitrator. The names and addresses of all witnesses and exhibits in order received shall be made a part of the record.

The arbitrator may vary the normal procedure under which the initiating party first presents its claim, but in any case shall afford full and equal opportunity to all parties for the presentation of relevant proofs.

27. Arbitration in the Absence of a Party

Unless the law provides to the contrary, the arbitration may proceed in the absence of any party who, after due notice, fails to be present or fails to obtain an adjournment. An award shall not be made solely on the default of a party. The arbitrator shall require the other party to submit such evidence as may be required for the making of an award.

28. Evidence

The parties may offer such evidence as they desire and shall produce such additional evidence as the arbitrator may deem necessary to an understanding and determination of the dispute. An arbitrator authorized by law to subpoena witnesses and documents may do so independently or upon the request of any party. The arbitrator shall be the judge of the relevance and materiality of the evidence offered and conformity to legal rules of evidence shall not be necessary. All evidence shall be taken in the presence of all of the arbitrators and all of the parties except where any of the parties is absent in default or has waived the right to be present.

29. Evidence by Affidavit and Filing of Documents

The arbitrator may receive and consider the evidence of witnesses by affidavit, giving it only such weight as seems proper after consideration of any objection made to its admission.

All documents that are not filed with the arbitrator at the hearing, but arranged at the hearing or subsequently by agreement of the parties to be submitted, shall be filed with the AAA for transmission to the arbitrator. All parties shall be afforded opportunity to examine such documents.

30. Inspection

Whenever the arbitrator deems it necessary, he or she may make an inspection in connection with the subject matter of the dispute after written notice to the parties, who may, if they so desire, be present at such inspection.

31. Closing of Hearings

The arbitrator shall inquire of all parties whether they have any further proofs to offer or witnesses to be heard. Upon receiving negative replies, the arbitrator shall declare the hearings closed and a minute thereof shall be recorded. If briefs or other documents are to be filed, the hearings shall be declared closed as of the final date set by the arbitrator for filing with the AAA. The time limit within which the arbitrator is required to make an award shall commence to run, in the absence of another agreement by the parties, upon the closing of the hearings.

32. Reopening of Hearings

The hearings may for good cause shown be reopened by the arbitrator at will or on the motion of either party at any time before the award is made, but, if the reopening of the hearings would prevent the making of the award within the specific time agreed upon by the parties in the contract out of which the controversy has arisen, the matter may not be reopened unless both parties agree upon the extension of such time. When no specific date is fixed in the contract, the arbitrator may reopen the hearings and shall have thirty days from the closing of the reopened hearings within which to make an award.

33. Waiver of Oral Hearings

The parties may provide, by written agreement, for the waiver of oral hearings. If the parties are unable to agree as to the procedure, the AAA shall specify a fair and equitable procedure.

34. Waiver of Rules

Any party who proceeds with the arbitration after knowledge that any provision or requirement of these rules has not been complied with and who fails to state an objection thereto in writing shall be deemed to have waived the right to object.

35. Extensions of Time

The parties may modify any period of time by mutual agreement. The AAA may for good cause extend any period of time established by these rules, except the time for making the award. The AAA shall notify the parties of any such extension of time and its reason therefor.

36. Serving of Notice

Each party to a Submission or other agreement that provides for arbitration under these rules shall be deemed to have consented and shall consent that any papers, notices, or process necessary or proper for the initiation or continuation of an arbitration under these rules; for any court action in connection therewith; or for the entry of judgment on an award made thereunder may be served upon such party by mail addressed to such party or its attorney at the last known address or by personal service, within or without the state wherein the arbitration is to be held.

37. Time of Award
The award shall be rendered promptly by the arbitrator and, unless otherwise agreed by the parties or specified by law, no later than thirty days from the date of closing the hearings or, if oral hearings have been waived, from the date of transmitting the final statements and proofs to the arbitrator.

38. Form of Award
The award shall be in writing and shall be signed either by the neutral arbitrator or by a concurring majority if there be more than one arbitrator. The parties shall advise the AAA whenever they do not require the arbitrator to accompany the award with an opinion.

39. Award upon Settlement
If the parties settle their dispute during the course of the arbitration, the arbitrator may, upon their request, set forth the terms of the agreed settlement in an award.

40. Delivery of Award to Parties
Parties shall accept as legal delivery of the award the placing of the award or a true copy thereof in the mail by the AAA, addressed to such party at its last known address or to its attorney; personal service of the award; or the filing of the award in any other manner that may be prescribed by law.

41. Release of Documents for Judicial Proceedings
The AAA shall, upon the written request of a party, furnish to such party, at its expense, certified facsimiles of any papers in the AAA's possession that may be required in judicial proceedings relating to the arbitration.

42. Judicial Proceedings and Exclusion of Liability
(a) Neither the AAA nor any arbitrator in a proceeding under these rules is a necessary party in judicial proceedings relating to the arbitration.

(b) Neither the AAA nor any arbitrator shall be liable to any party for any act or omission in connection with any arbitration conducted under these rules.

43. Administrative Fees

As a not-for-profit organization, the AAA shall prescribe an administrative fee schedule to compensate it for the cost of providing administrative services. The schedule in effect at the time of filing shall be applicable.

44. Expenses

The expenses of witnesses for either side shall be paid by the party producing such witnesses.

Expenses of the arbitration, other than the cost of the stenographic record, including required traveling and other expenses of the arbitrator and of AAA representatives and the expenses of any witness or the cost of any proof produced at the direct request of the arbitrator, shall be borne equally by the parties, unless they agree otherwise, or unless the arbitrator, in the award, assesses such expenses or any part thereof against any specified party or parties.

45. Communication with Arbitrator

There shall be no communication between the parties and a neutral arbitrator other than at oral hearings. Any other oral or written communication from the parties to the arbitrator shall be directed to the AAA for transmittal to the arbitrator.

46. Interpretation and Application of Rules

The arbitrator shall interpret and apply these rules insofar as they relate to the arbitrator's powers and duties. When there is more than one arbitrator and a difference arises among them concerning the meaning or application of any such rule, it shall be decided by a majority vote. If that is unobtainable, the arbitrator or either party may refer the question to the AAA for final decision. All other rules shall be interpreted and applied by the AAA.

Streamlined Labor Arbitration Rules

Initiation of Arbitration

Cases may be initiated by joint submission in writing, or in accordance with a collective bargaining agreement.

Appointment of Arbitrator

The arbitrator will be appointed by the AAA from members of its Panel of Labor Arbitrators who have agreed to serve under these rules.

Scheduling of Hearings

The hearing shall be held within 25 days of appointment of the arbitrator. The arbitrator shall fix the time and place of hearing, notice of which shall be given to the parties by the AAA at least five calendar days in advance.

No Transcripts and Briefs

There shall be no briefs or transcripts.

Award

The award is due within five business days of the closing of the hearing. The opinion will be brief and generally not exceed two pages in length.

Judicial Proceedings and Exclusion of Liability

(a) Neither the AAA nor any arbitrator in a proceeding under these rules is a necessary party in judicial proceedings relating to the arbitration.

(b) Neither the AAA nor any arbitrator shall be liable to any party for any act or omission in connection with any arbitration conducted under these rules.

Interpretation and Application of Rules

Any questions not covered by these rules shall be decided in accordance with the Voluntary Labor Arbitration Rules of the American Arbitration Association.

The arbitrator shall interpret and apply these rules insofar as they relate to the arbitrator's powers and duties. All other rules shall be interpreted and applied by the AAA, as administrator.

American Arbitration Association Offices

Atlanta (30309–3214) • India Johnson
1360 Peachtree Street, NE, Suite 270 •
(404) 872-3022/881-1134 (Fax)

Boston (02110–1703) • Richard M. Reilly
133 Federal Street • (617) 451-6600/451-0763 (Fax)

Charlotte (28202–2431) • Neil Carmichael
428 East Fourth Street, Suite 300 •
(704) 347-0200/347-2804 (Fax)

Chicago (60606–1212) • David Scott Carfello
205 West Wacker Drive, Suite 1100 •
(312) 346-2282/346-0135 (Fax)

Cincinnati (45202–2809) • Philip S. Thompson
441 Vine Street, Suite 3308 • (513) 241-8434/241-8437 (Fax)

**Cleveland (Middleburg Heights 44130–3490) •
Audrey Mendenhall**
17900 Jefferson Road, Suite 101 • (216) 891-4741/891-4740 (Fax)

Dallas (75240–6620) • Helmut O. Wolff
Two Galleria Tower, Suite 1440 • (214) 702-8222/490-9008 (Fax)

Denver (80264–2101) • Mark Appel
1660 Lincoln Street, Suite 2150 • (303) 831-0823/832-3626 (Fax)

Garden City, NY (11530–4789) • Mark A. Resnick
585 Stewart Avenue, Suite 302 • (516) 222-1660/745-6447 (Fax)

Hartford (06106–1943) • Karen M. Jalkut
Two Hartford Square West • (203) 278-5000/246-8442 (Fax)

Honolulu (96813–4714) • Keith W. Hunter
810 Richards Street, Suite 641 • (808) 531-0541/533-2306 (Fax)
In Guam: (671) 477-1845/477-3178 (Fax)

Houston (77002–6707) • **Therese Tilley**
1001 Fannin Street, Suite 1317 •
(713) 739–1302/739–1702 (Fax)

Kansas City, MO (64106–2110) • **Lori A. Madden**
1101 Walnut Street, Suite 903 • (816) 221–6401/471–5264 (Fax)

Los Angeles (90020–0994) • **Jerrold L. Murase**
443 Shatto Place • (213) 383–6516/386–2251 (Fax)

Miami (33131–2501) • **René Grafals**
99 SE Fifth Street, Suite 200 • (305) 358–7777/358–4931 (Fax)

Michigan (Southfield 48034–7405) • **Mary A. Bedikian**
Ten Oak Hollow Street, Suite 170 • (313)352–5500/352–3147 (Fax)

Minneapolis (55402–1092) • **James R. Deye**
514 Nicollet Mall, Suite 670 • (612) 332–6545/342–2334 (Fax)

Nashville (37219–2111) •
221 Fourth Avenue North • (615) 256–5857/244–8570 (Fax)

New Jersey (Somerset 08873–4120) • **Richard Naimark**
265 Davidson Avenue, Suite 140 • (908) 560–9560/560–8850 (Fax)

New Orleans (70130–6101) • **Deann Gladwell**
650 Poydras Street, Suite 1535 • (504) 522–8781/561–8041 (Fax)

New York (10020–1203) • **Carolyn M. Penna**
140 West 51st Street • (212) 484–4000/307–4387 (Fax)

Orange County, CA (Irvine 92714–6220) • **Lori S. Markowicz**
2601 Main Street, Suite 240 • (714) 474–5090/474–5087 (Fax)

Orlando (32801–2742) • **Mark Sholander**
201 East Pine Street, Suite 800 • (407) 648–1185/649–8668 (Fax)

Philadelphia (19102–4106) • **Kenneth Egger**
230 South Broad Street, Floor 6 • (215) 732–5260/732–5002 (Fax)

Phoenix (85012–2365) • **Deborah Krell-Schindler**
333 E. Osborn Road, Suite 310 • (602) 234–0950/230–2151 (Fax)

Pittsburgh (15222–1207) • **John F. Schano**
Four Gateway Center, Room 419 • (412)261–3617/261–6055 (Fax)

Providence (02903) • **Mark Bayliss**
115 Cedar Street • (401) 453–3250/453–6194 (Fax)

St. Louis (63101–1614) • **Neil Moldenhauer**
One Mercantile Center, Suite 2512 •
(314) 621–7175/621–3730 (Fax)

Salt Lake City (84111–3834) • Kimberly L. Curtis
645 South 200 East, Suite 203 •
(801) 531–9748/531–0660 (Fax)

San Diego (92101–5278) • Dennis Sharp
525 C Street, Suite 400 • (619) 239–3051/239–3807 (Fax)

San Francisco (94104–1113) • Charles A. Cooper
417 Montgomery Street • (415) 981–3901/781–8426 (Fax)

Seattle (98101–2511) • Neal M. Blacker
1325 Fourth Avenue, Suite 1414
(206) 622–6435/343–5679 (Fax)

Syracuse (13202–1376) • Deborah A. Brown
205 South Salina Street • (315) 472–5483/472–0966 (Fax)

Washington, DC (20036–4104) • Garylee Cox
1150 Connecticut Avenue, NW, 6th Floor
(202) 296–8510/872–9574 (Fax)

White Plains, NY (10601–4485) • Marion J. Zinman
34 South Broadway • (914) 946–1119/946–2661 (Fax)

National Representative, Washington, DC (20036) • Thomas R. Colosi
1730 Rhode Island Avenue, NW, Suite 512 •
(202) 331–7073